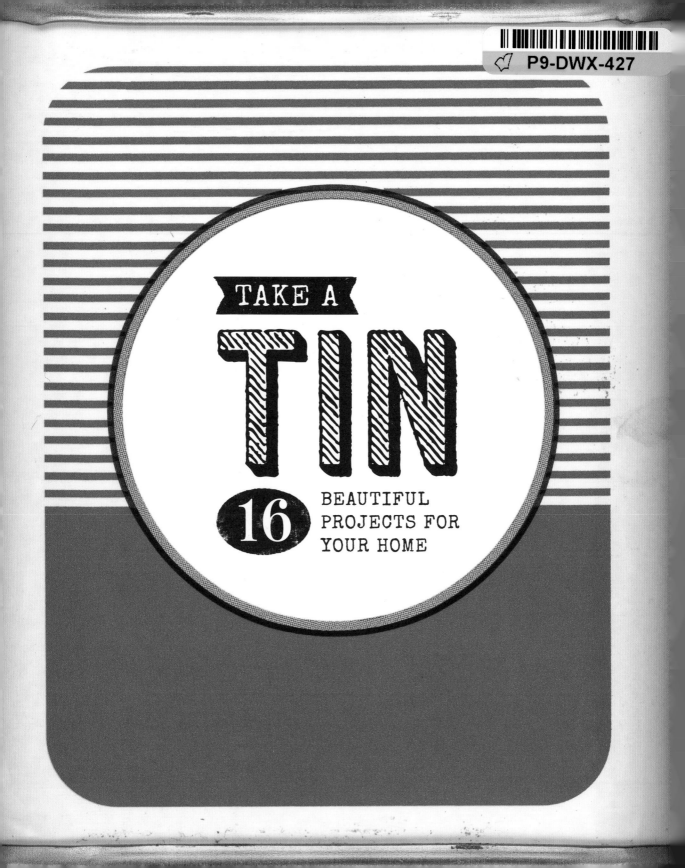

TAKE A

TIN

16 BEAUTIFUL PROJECTS FOR YOUR HOME

TAKE A
TIN

16 BEAUTIFUL PROJECTS FOR YOUR HOME

Jemima Schlee

First published 2016 by
Guild of Master Craftsman Publications Ltd
Castle Place, 166 High Street, Lewes,
East Sussex BN7 1XU

Text © Jemima Schlee, 2016
Copyright in the Work © GMC Publications Ltd, 2016

ISBN 978 1 78494 110 9

The publishers and author can accept no legal
responsibility for any consequences arising from
the application of information, advice or instructions
given in this publication. A catalogue record for this
book is available from the British Library.

Publisher Jonathan Bailey
Production Manager Jim Bulley
Senior Project Editors Virginia Brehaut and
Dominique Page
Editor Robin Pridy
Managing Art Editor Gilda Pacitti
Art Editor Luana Gobbo
Step Photography Jemima Schlee
Photographer Emma Sekhon

Colour origination by GMC Reprographics
Printed and bound in China

For Harrison
and Martha

Contents

Pendant Light p.62

Tiered Storage Stand p.44

Desk Lamp p.52

Heart Votives p.58

Introduction	8
Gallery	10

STORAGE
Labelled Storage Tins	28
Magnetic Pinboard	32
Box Pincushion	38
Tiered Storage Stand	44

LIGHTING
Desk Lamp	52
Heart Votives	58
Pendant Light	62
Brioche-tin Candles	66

DECORATIONS
Blossom Wreath	72
Cookie-cutter Chimes	78
Picture Frame	82
Disc Decorations	88

GIFTS
Cress-growing Kit	94
Memory Tin	98
Ring-pull Bracelet	106
Travel Games	112
Techniques	116
Templates	130
Suppliers/Acknowledgements	134
Index	135

Magnetic Pinboard p.32

Cookie-cutter Chimes p.78

Brioche-tin Candles p.66

Travel Games p.112

Box Pincushion p.38

Picture Frame p.82

INTRODUCTION

Tin cans come in many shapes and sizes, some with designs printed on their surface, others wrapped in paper labels. With a little ingenuity they can be turned into items for your home and garden. Here are 16 projects to make for everyday use or special occasions.

PRESERVING FOOD in tin cans has a long history. From as early as 1772, the Dutch Navy preserved its freshly caught salmon in tin-plated iron boxes. By the early 1800s, Frenchman Philippe de Girard had patented the first tin can. The world's first commercial canning factory opened in London in 1813 and by 1901, the American Can Company had opened its doors. These first tins were solid, weighing more than their contents, and instructions on them read: 'cut round the top near the outer edge with a chisel and hammer'.

Today's tins are made of thin metal, most simply requiring one end to be pierced, or completely removed with a tin opener to reveal their contents. Some have ring-pulls, some have keys you battle with to unwind as you splash yourself with oil. But these stalwarts of the grocery cupboard remain barely changed, as has the basic structure of the classic, ribbed tin can.

Tin cans evoke childhood memories of building camps, communicating by tin-can telephone and wobbling about on tin-can stilts with ever-short string handles.

This page:
Labelled Storage Tins **page 28**
Opposite:
Magnetic Pinboard **page 32**

Opposite:
Box Pincushion
page 38
This page:
Tiered Storage Stand
page 44

This page:
Desk Lamp **page 52**
Opposite:
Heart Votives **page 58**

This page: Pendant Light **page 62**
Opposite: Brioche-tin Candles **page 66**

Opposite: Blossom Wreath **page 72**
This page: Cookie-cutter Chimes **page 78**

Opposite: Picture Frame **page 82**
This page: Disc Decorations **page 88**

This page:
Cress-growing Kit **page** 94
Opposite: Memory Tin **page** 98

This page:
Ring-pull Bracelet **page 106**
Opposite:
Travel Games **page 112**

STORAGE

This is a quick and simple way to transform a food tin to create a useful container for pencils, crochet hooks or paintbrushes. Crochet a cover in fine cotton and embroider a personalized label in chain stitch with symbols, numbers or letters using scraps of yarn.

28 LABELLED STORAGE TINS

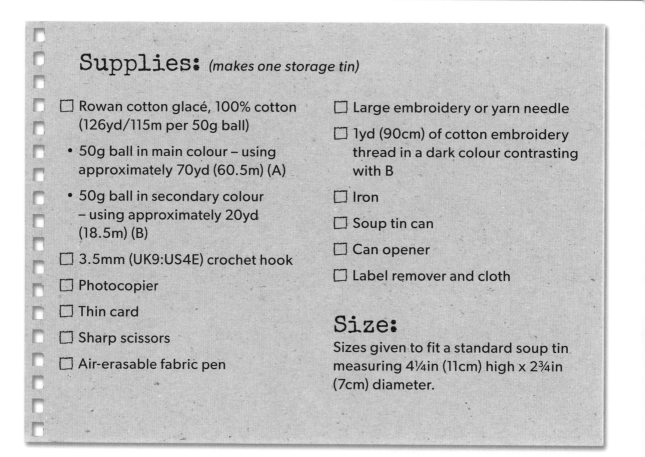

Supplies: *(makes one storage tin)*

- ☐ Rowan cotton glacé, 100% cotton (126yd/115m per 50g ball)
  - • 50g ball in main colour – using approximately 70yd (60.5m) (A)
  - • 50g ball in secondary colour – using approximately 20yd (18.5m) (B)
- ☐ 3.5mm (UK9:US4E) crochet hook
- ☐ Photocopier
- ☐ Thin card
- ☐ Sharp scissors
- ☐ Air-erasable fabric pen

- ☐ Large embroidery or yarn needle
- ☐ 1yd (90cm) of cotton embroidery thread in a dark colour contrasting with B
- ☐ Iron
- ☐ Soup tin can
- ☐ Can opener
- ☐ Label remover and cloth

Size:
Sizes given to fit a standard soup tin measuring 4¼in (11cm) high x 2¾in (7cm) diameter.

TENSION

24 sts and 26 rows to 4in (10cm) over double crochet on a 3.5mm hook. Use a larger or smaller hook if necessary to obtain the correct tension. The tension here is not crucial, but you should use a tension square (see page 126) – it will make all the difference for the snug fit you need over your can. For larger or smaller tins, adjust the number of stitches and lines you work in crochet, using the tension square to work out your figures.

Step 1

Create the crochet cover for the tin, as follows.

Foundation row: Using yarn A and your 3.5mm (UK9:US4E) crochet hook, make 55 ch, turn.
Row 1: 1 dc into 2nd ch from hook, 1 dc into remaining 53 ch, turn (54 sts).
Rows 2–4: 1 ch, 1 dc into each dc to end, turn.
Rows 5–24: 1 ch, 1 dc into next 18 dc, change to yarn (see Changing Colour, page 128) and dc into next 18 dc, change to yarn B and dc into remaining 18 dc, turn.
Rows 25–29: As row 2. Using B, cut the tail of your yarn to 8in (20cm) and pull through the loop left on your hook to finish off.

Step 2

Copy the template on page 131 onto thin card. Alternatively, draw and print out your own design to personalize your tin. Cut out with scissors.

TIP

IF YOU USE A LARGER OR SMALLER TIN, ADJUST THE SIZE OF THE NUMBER, LETTER OR SYMBOL TO FIT.

Step 3

Position the template centrally on your crochet and draw around it with a pen.

Step 4

Thread the embroidery or yarn needle with the embroidery thread and work in chain stitch to outline your design. Bring the thread through to the front of your work on your line **4a**. Insert the needle from where it emerged and bring the needle out ¼in (6mm) further along the stitch line, keeping the working thread under the needle's point as you do so. Pull the thread through, thus trapping a loop of thread to produce the chain **4b**. Repeat to complete the outline. End by inserting the needle through to the back of your work on the other side of the working thread to anchor it. Finish off with a few small, tight stitches.

Step 5

Press your crochet work on the wrong side with a hot iron. Thread the finishing yarn (A) tail through the embroidery or yarn needle, and with right sides facing, sew the two side edges together. Finish the yarn end off with a couple of small stitches, one on top of the other, before running the yarn through the back of a couple of stitches and trimming it flush.

Step 6

Using a can opener, remove the lid inside the top rim of the tin so that the container has no sharp edges. Clean the tin and remove any labels or glue with label remover, then slip your cover over the outside.

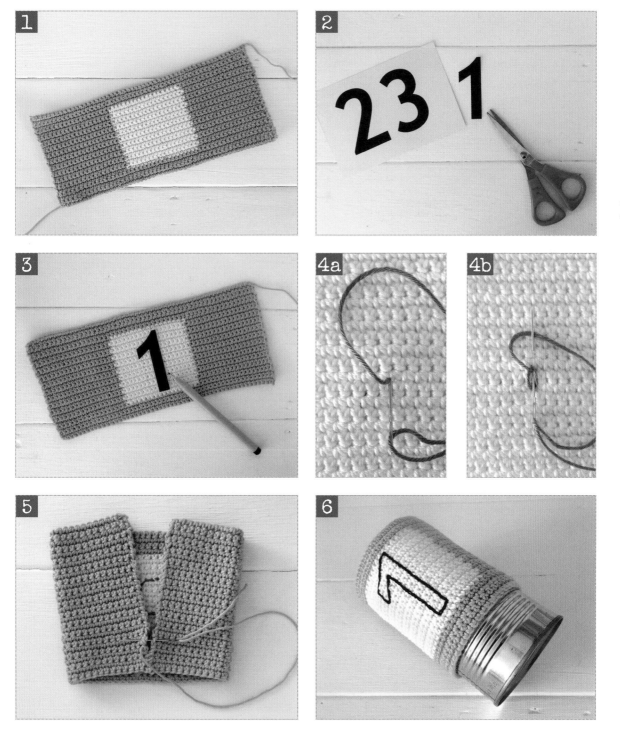

Transform a baking tray into a magnetic pinboard with useful tin 'pockets' to store essentials and clear a little extra space on your desk. Use bulldog clips and different-sized tins, covering them with decorative papers to corral notes and receipts.

MAGNETIC PINBOARD

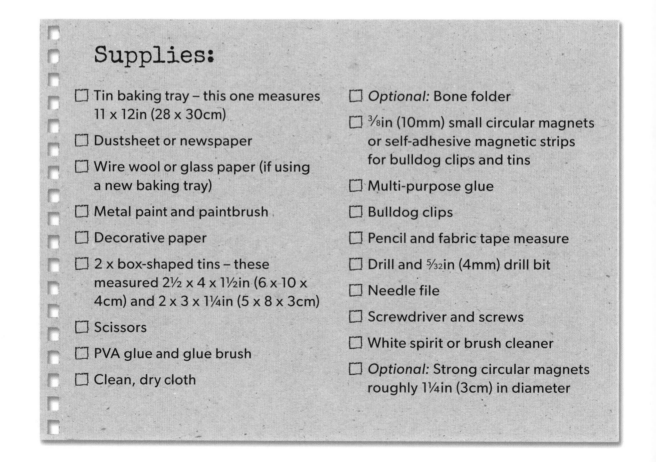

Supplies:

- [ ] Tin baking tray – this one measures 11 x 12in (28 x 30cm)
- [ ] Dustsheet or newspaper
- [ ] Wire wool or glass paper (if using a new baking tray)
- [ ] Metal paint and paintbrush
- [ ] Decorative paper
- [ ] 2 x box-shaped tins – these measured 2½ x 4 x 1½in (6 x 10 x 4cm) and 2 x 3 x 1¼in (5 x 8 x 3cm)
- [ ] Scissors
- [ ] PVA glue and glue brush
- [ ] Clean, dry cloth
- [ ] *Optional:* Bone folder
- [ ] ⅜in (10mm) small circular magnets or self-adhesive magnetic strips for bulldog clips and tins
- [ ] Multi-purpose glue
- [ ] Bulldog clips
- [ ] Pencil and fabric tape measure
- [ ] Drill and 5/32in (4mm) drill bit
- [ ] Needle file
- [ ] Screwdriver and screws
- [ ] White spirit or brush cleaner
- [ ] *Optional:* Strong circular magnets roughly 1¼in (3cm) in diameter

Step 1

Prepare the baking tray for painting, laying down a dust sheet or newspaper beneath it and making sure it is grease-free and dry by wiping it with white spirit or brush cleaner. If new, rub it with wire wool or glass paper to key the surface. Apply several thin coats of metal paint, leaving drying time in between. If the tray's lipped edge is fairly raised, give the outside edges and sides of the back a good covering too, but not the back itself. Alternatively, use several thin coats of spray paint.

Step 2

For the paper-covered pockets, cut a strip of paper that measures the exact height of the tin plus about ¼in (6mm) to fold in at the top edge, by the width of its circumference plus ⅜in (10mm) for an overlap at the back. Cover half the back, both sides and the front of the tin with glue. Use a stabbing action with a stiff glue brush – this will help the paper to lie smoothly and reduce wrinkles.

Starting at the centre back, wrap the strip of paper around the tin, positioning the bottom edge snugly against the bottom lip of the tin, and leaving the overhang of ¼in (6mm) protruding beyond the top edge. Use a clean, dry cloth to smooth any wrinkles in the paper and to ensure even contact with the tin. Be careful not to stretch the paper while doing this – if the paper is thin, the glue will make it damp and more fragile.

Step 3

Apply glue to the remaining length of the paper, again using a stabbing action with the brush, and smooth it onto the final half of the back of the tin using your cloth, overlapping the leading edge by ⅜in (10mm). With a damp cloth, quickly wipe away any excess glue that may ooze out at the join. Now apply glue to the inside of the paper over-hanging the open top of the tin.

Step 4

Use your fingers to fold the paper over the top edge, smoothing it out with a fingernail, or the end of a bone folder if you have one. Take a bit of time at the corners to keep any creases even and to a minimum.

Step 5

Setting the magnets ⅜in (10mm) from the top edge of the back surface of the tins, use multi-purpose glue to secure them to the back of the tin 'pockets'. Leave to dry fully, following the manufacturer's instructions.

TIP

IF STORING HEAVIER ITEMS, SUCH AS SCISSORS, FIX YOUR 'POCKET' TINS WITH MORE THAN ONE LARGE MAGNET, OR WITH MULTI-PURPOSE GLUE.

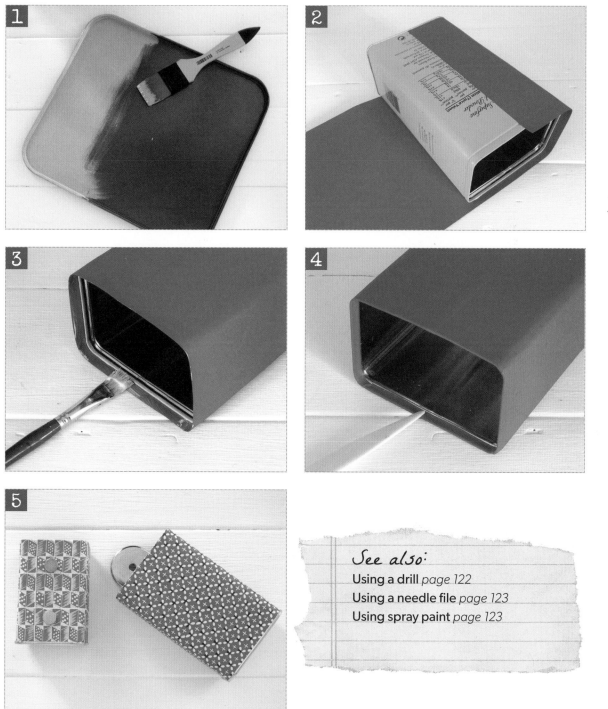

See also:
Using a drill *page 122*
Using a needle file *page 123*
Using spray paint *page 123*

Step 6

Take small scraps of paper and cut them to strips the exact width of your bulldog clips.

Step 7

Use a fabric tape measure to measure the distance across the top of the clip (A) and down to the opening edge of one side (B), as shown above. Cut a piece of your paper strip to this measurement plus ¼in (6mm). Cut a slit in the paper at distance A from the top edge and use a pencil to mark a dotted line at distance B on the back of the paper. Apply glue to the back of the paper, again using a stabbing action.

Step 8

Slot one of the arms of the clip through the slit. Smooth the paper along the top, and down the front of the clip.

Step 9

Pinch the clip open and fold the last ¼in (6mm) of glued paper around the open edge and smooth it down. Clip it onto a wedge of folded paper to hold this end of the paper firmly in position while the glue dries fully.

Step 10

Apply multi-purpose glue, or attach circular magnets or a piece of self-adhesive magnetic strip to the back of the bulldog clips.

Step 11

Starting with the tray laid out vertically in front of you, take time to carefully position the tins and clips. Once you are happy with the layout, mark two places that will be covered by the containers and clips, one near the top and one near the bottom.

Step 12

Drill two ⁵⁄₃₂in (4mm) holes at your marks. Use the needle file to take off any sharp edges or burrs.

Step 13

Lastly, screw the tray to a wall or cupboard door and position the tins and clips to cover the screw holes. Attach the tins by their magnets, or by slipping a strong magnet inside them – the strength of the magnet will dictate the load you can put into the tin. The clips will hold with the magnets, glue or magnetic strip you attached to them at Step 10.

DRILL SAFETY
When using a drill to make holes in metal, always be sure to use protective goggles and gloves to avoid cuts and flying pieces of tin.

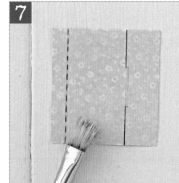

A cute little pincushion firmly perched on the lid of a storage tin
is practical in more ways than one and makes the perfect gift.
You can make this in any size and, satisfyingly, use the smallest,
most precious scraps of fabric and ribbon you've been saving.

BOX PINCUSHION

Supplies: *(makes one pincushion)*

- A tin with a lid – this one measures 4¼ x 3 x 1in (11 x 8 x 2.5cm)
- Card, pencil and ruler
- Sharp scissors
- Bradawl or small knitting needle
- Fabric 1⅜in (3cm) larger all round than the lid of your tin
- Sewing thread
- Sewing needle and pins
- *Optional:* sewing machine
- *Optional:* heavyweight sewing thread (jeans stitching weight)

- A few large handfuls of hollow-fibre stuffing
- Cotton embroidery thread in a contrasting colour to your fabric
- 2 x small buttons
- Multi-purpose glue
- String
- Ribbon or trim – the circumference of your tin plus ⅜in (10mm)
- Paper
- Bone folder or large knitting needle
- Felt – enough to cover the bottom of the tin

Step 1

Draw around the top of the tin onto a piece of card. Cut out this template slighter smaller – about $\frac{1}{16}$in (2mm) – inside your drawn line. Check that the card fits on the top of the tin, laying just a fraction smaller all the way around. Draw a line, left to right, across the centre of the piece of card. Use a bradawl or a small knitting needle to make two holes on this line, equally spaced along it to divide the line into thirds – here, it is roughly $1\frac{3}{8}$in (3.5cm) from either end.

Step 2

Draw around the tin lid again. Make yourself a rectangular template 1in (2.5cm) larger all the way around and use it as a pattern to cut out the pad fabric. Stitch $1\frac{3}{8}$in (3cm) in from the fabric's raw edge. If using a sewing machine, use your longest stitch and extra-thick bobbin thread. If hand stitching, make $\frac{1}{4}$in (6mm) long running stitches and use your thread doubled.

TIP

IF YOUR TIN IS PRINTED, YOU COULD RUB THE BASE WITH WIRE WOOL OR SPRAY PAINT IT (SEE PAGE 123) AT STEP 2, OR TAKE INSPIRATION FROM ITS COLOURS TO HELP YOU CHOOSE YOUR FABRIC, THREAD AND BUTTONS.

Step 3

If you have used a sewing machine, thread one tail end of the thicker thread (from the bobbin) onto a needle and make several overlapping stitches by hand to secure this end firmly to the fabric. Remove the needle and cut this thread end to about $\frac{3}{8}$in (10mm).

Step 4

Now thread the needle onto the other tail end of the thick thread. Pull the thread firmly to draw and gather the outside edge of the fabric towards the middle **4a** At the same time, start filling the pad with the hollow fibre stuffing **4b**.

Step 5

When the pincushion pad is fairly full, slot the card under the gathered edges. Continue stuffing between the fabric and the card. When you are happy with the density of the stuffing, give the thread a final tug and smooth out the gathering around the edges and corners of the card. Secure the gathering with several firm stitches, one on top of another, to hold it permanently. Remove the needle and cut the thread end to about $\frac{3}{8}$in (10mm).

Step 6

Thread your needle with embroidery thread. Knot one end and, with your work laid horizontally, make one small stitch at the left-hand edge of the underside of the cushion.

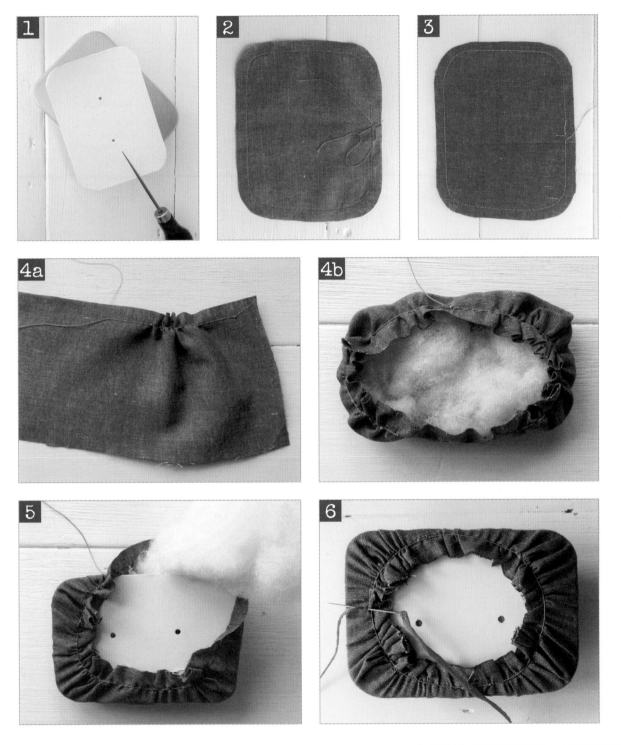

Step 7

Turn your work so that it lies vertically in front
of you. Wrap the thread downwards, around
the plump cushion side, and back over the top
to the underside of the cushion again. Now insert
the needle through the bottom/lower hole in the
card through to the front.

Step 8

With the front of the work facing you, pull the thread
from behind through to the front of the cushion and
give it a firm tug. Wrap the thread around the pad
to the right, around the back and to the front from
the left-hand side. Push the needle from the front
to the back, through the same hole. Keep the
tension firm, thus creating two plump sections on
the top of the cushion.

Step 9

Keeping a firm tension in your thread, push the
needle back up through the top hole to the front.
Repeat the thread wrapping at the top of the
cushion before making a few stitches at the back,
one on top of another, to retain the six plump
segments you have created on the front of the
cushion pad. Stitch two small buttons where

the threads cross each other at the front of the pad,
tugging the thread securely before finishing with
a few overlapping stitches at the back.

Step 10

Following the manufacturer's instructions, apply
multi-purpose glue to both the bottom of the
pincushion pad and the top surface of the tin lid.
After a couple of minutes, position the pad carefully
on the lid and use string to tie it securely in position
until the glue has fully set.

Step 11

Cut a piece of ribbon or trim about ⅜in (10mm)
longer than the lid's circumference. Run glue
around its outside edge where the pincushion joins
it. Starting between the two hinges where the lid
is attached to the box, stick the trim firmly along
the join, finishing it off with another dot of glue at
the overlap and giving it a good press to ensure it's
smoothly and evenly attached all the way around.

Step 12

When the ribbon has completely dried, open the
box and make a template for the inside of it. Cut a
rough rectangle of paper slightly larger than the tin
all the way around and push it down into the bottom.
Use a bone folder or a large knitting needle to push
the paper into the sides and corners, making a clear
fold or crease in it all the way around.

Step 13

Cut around the creases in the paper and use this
template to cut a piece of felt to drop into and
perfectly fit and line the base of your tin.

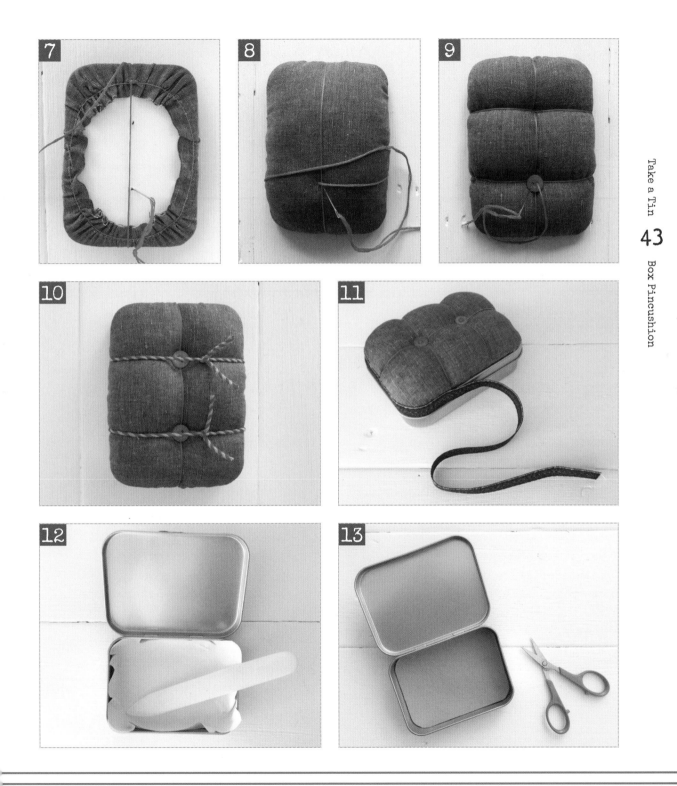

The crafter's take on a cake stand, this has a special lidded tin
to store string in at the top and is made with cake and cookie tins. You can
combine any number of bases, lids and tins, mixing and matching them
to store your collection of sewing materials and equipment.

44 TIERED STORAGE STAND

Supplies:

- Assorted cake or cookie tins with lids: I used an 8in (20cm) diameter base, 6¾in (17cm) diameter lid and 5¼in (13.5cm) diameter base
- Treacle/syrup tin with lid, 3in high x 3in diameter (8cm high x 8cm in diameter)
- ½–⅜in (13–10mm) chrome reducer (**A**) (see page 46)
- ⅜in (10mm) chrome rod, 4in (10cm) long, with thread at each end (**B**) (see page 46)
- ⅜in (10mm) chrome coupler (**C**) (see page 46)
- ⅜in (10mm) chrome rod, 6in (15cm) long, with thread at each end (**D**) (see page 46)
- 4 x ⅜in (10mm) chrome lock nut (**E**) (see page 46)
- 5 x 1½in (4cm) washers with ⅜in (10mm) holes (**F**) (see page 46)
- Permanent marker
- Drill and ⅜in (10mm) drill bit
- ⅜in (10mm) eyelet
- Hammer or eyelet pliers
- Needle file or emery paper
- Flat-nose pliers

ASSEMBLING HARDWARE

A ½–⅜in (13–10mm) chrome reducer

B ⅜in (10mm) chrome rod, 4in (10cm) long, with thread at each end

C ⅜in (10mm) chrome coupler

D ⅜in (10mm) chrome rod, 6in (15cm) long, with thread at each end

E ⅜in (10mm) chrome lock nut

F 1½in (4cm) washer with ³/₈in (10mm) holes

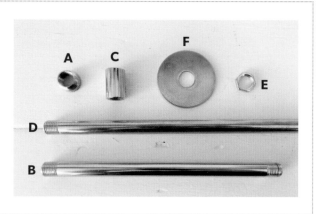

Step 1

Spend some time arranging the tins before laying the assembling elements in order. Left to right, these go as follows: **E** – **F** – larger tin – **F** – **E** – **D** – **E** – **F** – tin lid – **F** – **C** – **B** – **E** – **F** – medium tin – treacle/syrup tin – **A**.

Step 2

Make the string-holding tin for the top layer of your stand. Remove the lid from the syrup tin and find its centre, marking it with a permanent pen. Use a ⅜in (10mm) drill bit to drill a hole in the centre of the lid and the base.

Step 3

Following the eyelet manufacturer's instructions, insert and fix an eyelet in the hole in the lid using a hammer. I cut the eyelet punch that came in my kit in half, as it did not reach the centre hole of my lid's tin when folded in half for use (you can also use a pair of heavy-duty, long-reaching eyelet pliers).

TIP

WHEN ARRANGING THE TINS, USE UPTURNED GLASSES OR JARS ROUGHLY 4IN (10CM) AND 6IN (15CM) HIGH TO HELP YOU DECIDE ON THE ORDER OF YOUR TINS' LAYERS.

DRILL SAFETY

When using a drill to make holes in metal, always be sure to use protective goggles and gloves to avoid cuts and flying pieces of tin.

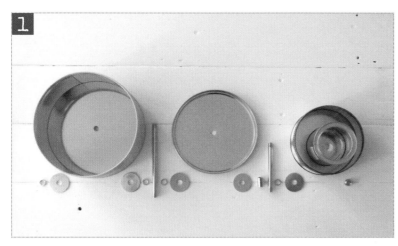

TIP

WHEN STORING THE STRING, DRAW
THE TAIL FROM THE CENTRE OF THE
BALL THROUGH THE EYELET HOLE
IN THE SYRUP TIN BEFORE PRESSING
DOWN THE LID. THIS MINIMIZES
THE CHANCES OF IT TANGLING
EXCESSIVELY INSIDE THE TIN.

See also:
Making holes using eyelet pliers
    page 122
Using a drill *page 122*
Using a needle file *page 123*

Step 4

Find and mark the centres of each of the tin lids and bases depending on your design. Drill ⅜in (10mm) holes in the tins at the marked centres. Finish off any burrs with a needle file or emery paper.

Step 5

Using the assembling elements, put the stand together, starting at the base. Screw a lock nut (**E**) onto one end of the 6in (15cm) rod (**D**) then slot a washer (**F**) onto the thread end next to the nut.

Step 6

Push the same end through the hole at the centre of the bottom tin from the inside, so that the short thread end protrudes at what will be the stand's bottom. Place another washer (**F**) onto the protruding thread and screw another lock nut (**E**) onto the end. Adjust the two lock nuts so that the one end is flush with the end of the rod's thread. Turn the nut as tightly as it will go, using flat-nose pliers if necessary. Sit the base tin on a flat surface to check that the final nut does not protrude further than the rim around the outside of the tin – your stand will wobble if so. Adjust both nuts if necessary.

Step 7

With the base tin sitting on the table, add another lock nut (**E**) to the top thread of the rod, and then another washer (**F**).

Step 8

Put together the top part of your tiered storage. Screw a lock nut (**E**) onto one end of your 4in (10cm) rod (**B**) and then slot a washer (**F**) onto the thread end after the nut. Push the same end through the hole at the bottom of your top tin from underneath, and then through the syrup tin's bottom, so that the short thread end protrudes inside at the bottom of what will be the string holder. Place a reducer (**A**) onto the protruding thread and screw it down. Turn the nut as tightly as it will go, using flat-nosed pliers if necessary.

Step 9

Now join the two halves of your storage. Slot the middle tin onto the top of the rod from Step 6. Add another washer (**F**) before screwing on a coupler (**C**). Finally, screw the bottom of the rod from Step 7 to the top of the joiner (**A**) and give all the joints and nuts a good tightening with your pliers.

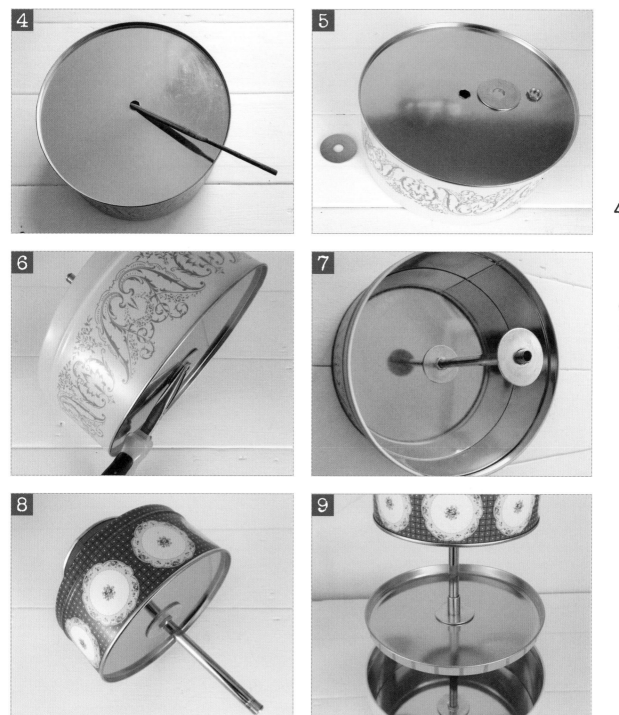

LIGHTING

This adjustable desk or bedside lamp has a lovely retro feel. I couldn't resist making a feature of this beautiful printed anchovy tin from a New York deli. Keep an eye out on your travels – home and abroad – for interesting tins with printed surfaces rather than paper labels.

DESK LAMP

Supplies:

- ☐ Electrical hardware: see page 54
- ☐ Can opener
- ☐ Tin, 5in (12.5cm) high and 4in (10cm) diameter, for the shade
- ☐ Tin, 2½in (6cm) high and 5in (12.5cm) diameter, for the base
- ☐ Label remover and cloth
- ☐ Drill with 1⅛in (2.8cm) drill bit (or to match the diameter of lampholder thread) and ⅜in (10mm) drill bit
- ☐ Safety goggles and gloves
- ☐ Tape measure
- ☐ Needle file and flat-nose pliers
- ☐ Masking tape
- ☐ Wire cutters and wire strippers
- ☐ Small screwdriver
- ☐ Plastic carrier bag
- ☐ Dustsheet or newspapers
- ☐ Spray paint
- ☐ Jigsaw and/or fretsaw
- ☐ 6 x 12in (15 x 30cm) MDF or wood
- ☐ Wood glue
- ☐ Fused plug with appropriate (lighting) ampage
- ☐ Lightbulb
- ☐ Three-core silk-covered earthed lighting cable to your desired length

ELECTRICAL HARDWARE

- **A** ½–⅜in (13–10mm) chrome reducer
- **B** ⅜in (10mm) cord grip
- **C** ⅜in (10mm) chrome couplers
- **D** BC (unswitched) lamp holder
- **E** ⅜in (10mm) lock nut
- **F** ⅜in (10mm) elbow/gas tap joints
- **G** 1½in (4cm) washers with ⅜in (10mm) holes
- **H** ⅜ x ½in (10 x 13mm) thread
- **I** ⅜in (10mm) chrome rod, 4in (10cm) long, with thread at each end
- **J** ⅜in (10mm) chrome rod, 10in (25cm) long, with thread at each end

Step 1

Make sure you have all the bits of electrical hardware you need (see list, above).

Step 2

Using a can opener, remove the top of the taller tin around the inside of the lid rim. Remove the bottom from the base tin, also around the inside of the rim. Clean the tins and, if necessary, remove any labels or glue with label remover. Drill a 1in (2.5cm) hole in the centre of the bottom of the tall tin and a ⅜in (10mm) hole in the centre of the top of the base tin.

DRILL SAFETY

When using a drill to make holes in metal, be sure to wear protective goggles and gloves to avoid cuts and flying pieces of tin.

Step 3

Drill a ⅜in (10mm) hole on the side of the base tin, ⅝in (1.5cm) up from the open bottom edge, then file the edges of all the holes with a needle file to remove any burrs left by the drill bit.

Step 4

Fix the cord grip (**B**) to the side of the base tin: push the screw end through the drilled hole from the outside and secure it with a lock nut (**E**) fixed firmly on the inside of the tin. Tighten the nut with pliers.

Step 5

Mark a point 25in (64cm) from one end of your wire cable and wrap a short length of tape around it – this measurement is the finished length of your lamp arm from the top of the base tin, plus 4in (10cm). Now remove the fabric covering from the 25in (64cm) length of the three wires from the taped marker.

Step 6

Start assembling the arm of the lamp. Lay out the relevant elements in order in front of you from left to right thus: **F** – **J** – **F** – **C** – **I** – **C** – **F** – **A** – **D**. Lay the cable down in front of you with the fabric-covered part of cable to your left and the uncovered wires to your right. Starting from the left, undo the first elbow/gas tap joint (**F**) and put the top half (the half with the screw hole) to one side. Feed all three wires through the back piece, ensuring the earth (green and yellow) wire lies around one side of the screw pin and the neutral (blue) and live (brown) pass around the other side.

Step 7

Feed the top half of the elbow/gas tap joint onto the three wires, replace the two small washers and screw the tap in tightly.

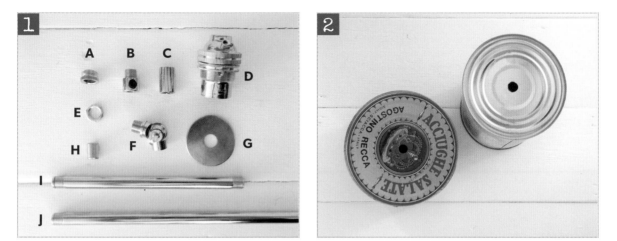

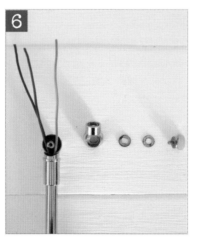

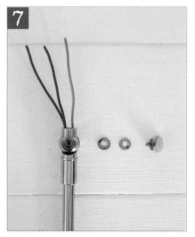

TIP

REMOVING THE COVERING
FROM THE WIRES MAKES
IT EASIER TO RUN THEM
THROUGH THE TUBES AND
JOINTS, ENSURING THE
EARTH WIRE IS SEPARATE
FROM THE LIVE AND
NEUTRAL AT THE JOINTS.

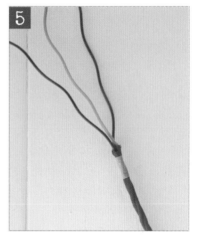

Step 8

Continue assembling the lamp arm by screwing on each element, working from left to right until the third elbow/gas tap joint (**F**) and the chrome reducer (**A**) are attached. Using wire cutters and strippers, trim the ends of the three wires and attach the lamp holder (**D**) following the manufacturer's instructions – make sure the lamp holder is firmly earthed at this point – this varies depending on the lamp holder, so do have it checked by a qualified electrician.

Step 9

Remove the holding ring from the lamp holder (**D**) and try slotting the tin shade on – if the fit is too tight, use a needle file to make it larger.

Step 10

Prepare your tin for painting. Line the inside with a plastic carrier bag, fixing it in position with several lengths of masking tape. Run the top edge of the tape just below the lip of the tin as evenly and neatly as you can. The bag and tape will mask the inside of the tin from paint. The inside of my tin was white; this, or a plain metal interior, will help to reflect the light once the lamp is assembled. Now paint the outside of the tin shade. When using spray paint, always work in a well-ventilated area and protect surrounding areas with a dustsheet or old newspaper. Apply numerous thin layers of paint with drying time allowed in between. Once dry, carefully peel away the masking tape from around the tin's inside edge and pull out the plastic bag to reveal a clean interior.

Step 11

Fix the lamp arm to the lamp base. Lay out the elements in order in front of you from left to right thus: **E** – **G** – **G**. Lay your work out in front of you with the assembled arm and shade on the right and the covered cable to your left. Working from right to left, thread a washer (**G**) along the cable. Now thread the cable through the hole on the top of the base tin to the inside. Thread the next washer (**G**) onto the cable, and then a nut (**E**). Working inside the tin, screw the nut next to the washer tightly against the tin, using pliers to achieve a snug fit.

Step 12

Loosen the screw on the cord grip (**B**) and feed the end of the cable through it from the inside to the outside of the tin. Tighten the screw firmly with a screwdriver.

Step 13

To counterbalance the weight of the top half of the lamp you need to weigh down the base tin. Using a jigsaw, cut two circles of MDF with diameters ⅛in (3mm) smaller than the diameter of your base tin. You can use the template on page 130, enlarging or reducing it on a photocopier to size if necessary. On each disc, drill a ⅜in (10mm) hole in the position marked on the template. Use a fret saw to remove the shaded areas.

Step 14

Glue the two discs together, ensuring the drilled holes align and slot the disc into the base tin, aligning the cut slot with the cable grip.

Step 15

Fix a plug to the end of the cable following the instructions and taking care to earth it securely. All you need to do now is to attach the shade, slotting it onto the lampholder thread and screwing the holding ring on tightly to hold it. Finally, screw in a light bulb.

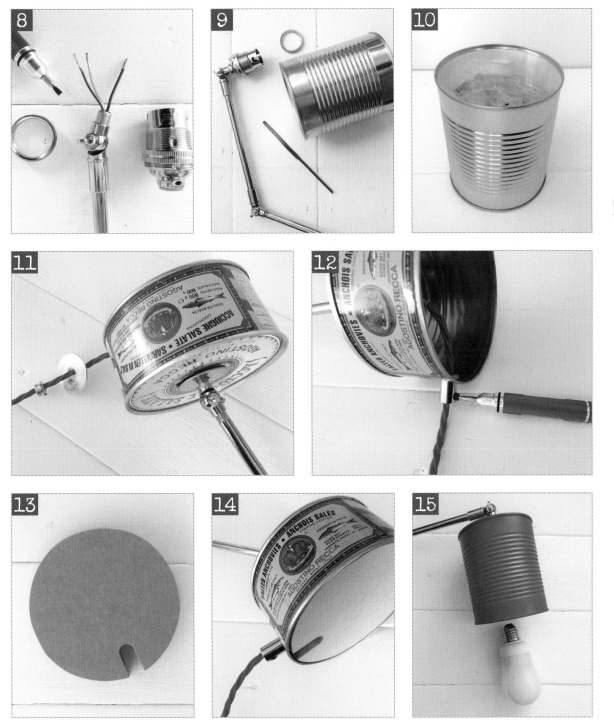

These heart votives are small versions of the traditional punched tin lantern. The little tea lights inside them twinkle and sparkle, bouncing off the cans' shiny metal interiors. Set a row of flickering tins along a mantelpiece or hang them in your porch at night.

HEART VOTIVES

Supplies: *(for one lantern and handle)*

- [ ] Tin can measuring roughly 3½in high x 3in diameter (9cm high x 7.5cm diameter)
- [ ] Can opener
- [ ] Label remover and cloth
- [ ] Access to a freezer
- [ ] The use of a photocopier, or a sheet of tracing paper and copier paper
- [ ] Scissors
- [ ] Masking (or Washi) tape
- [ ] Small towel or cloth
- [ ] Two nails of different diameters, roughly ¹⁄₃₂in (1mm) and ³⁄₃₂in (2.5mm)

- [ ] Hammer
- [ ] Scrap paper or plastic carrier bag
- [ ] Dustsheet or newspaper
- [ ] Spray paint
- [ ] 12in (30cm) of 1.25mm (SWG 18, AWG 16) gauge wire
- [ ] Wire cutters and round-nosed pliers

For the jig (optional):
- [ ] Jigsaw
- [ ] 5¾ x 8in (14 x 20cm) MDF
- [ ] Screwdriver
- [ ] 3 x nails and 2 x screws

Step 1

Using a can opener, remove the tin can lid inside the top rim so that the container has no sharp edges. Clean the tin and remove any labels and glue using label remover, then fill with water and leave in the freezer overnight until it has fully frozen.

Step 2

Photocopy or trace the template on page 131 and cut it out, altering the size as necessary. Wrap it around the tin and join the two ends with a strip of tape. Fold a cloth or towel to cushion the tin, then lay it on its side.

Step 3

Work methodically, using first the narrower nail to punch out the smaller dots, then the thicker nail to punch out the heart motifs and the two holes for the handle. A few taps with the hammer should suffice – don't hammer the nail in too far as it makes no difference to the hole size and makes it harder to pull the nail out.

Step 4

Remove the paper template and check the holes, making sure you haven't missed any. Leave the pierced tin in a sink until the ice has melted, or speed it up by running warm water over it.

See also:
Opening tin cans *page 120*
Making holes with a nail or punch
page 122
Using a needle file *page 123*
Using spray paint *page 123*

Step 5

If you want to paint your lantern, do so now. Stuff the tin with screwed-up scrap paper or a plastic bag to shield the inside of it from the paint.

Step 6

Use spray paint in several light layers, leaving drying time in between. Always use spray paints in a well-ventilated area – ideally outside – and protect the surrounding surfaces with a dustsheet or newspaper. Set aside to dry before removing the paper from inside.

Step 7

For a handful of lanterns, cut an 8½in (22cm) length of wire and use the pliers to bend it into the shape of the handle, with a small decorative loop at the top (see template on page 131). For a large number of lanterns, use a jig. Copy and cut out the template on page 131, then use a jigsaw to cut a 4½ x 5½in (12 x 14cm) rectangle of wood or board and a circle with a 2¾in (7cm) diameter. Screw the circle onto the rectangle with two screws, following the same wire-handle template as for freehand. For the top loop handle, hammer three nails into the board where indicated. Cut a 12in (30cm) length of wire and weave it around the screws and jig as shown, looping around the loop at the centre top as you go. Remove the wire from the jig and trim both ends about ³⁄₈in (10mm) from the bends at either end.

Step 8

To finish your lantern, hook either end of the handle through the punched holes from the inside to the outside, and use pliers to curl the ends of the wire to prevent them from slipping out of the holes.

TIP

YOU CAN ALSO PAINT
THE OUTSIDE OF
YOUR LANTERN BY
HAND WITH METAL
OR ENAMEL PAINT
AND A PAINTBRUSH.

Make simple, industrial-looking pendant lampshades from large catering food tins. Hang them in a row, low over a dining table, or in clusters at different heights. You can paint them in bold colours or trim them with bright pom-poms and beaded ribbon (see page 9).

PENDANT LIGHT

Supplies:

- [ ] Large tin – these ones measures 6in (15cm) in diameter and 7in (18cm) in height
- [ ] Can opener
- [ ] Label remover and soft, dry cloth
- [ ] Permanent marker
- [ ] Drill with 1⅛in (2.8cm) drill bit (or to match the diameter of your lampholder thread) and ¼in (6mm) drill bit (optional)
- [ ] Safety goggles and gloves
- [ ] Needle file
- [ ] Plastic carrier bag
- [ ] Masking tape

- [ ] Spray paint
- [ ] Dustsheet or newspaper
- [ ] White spirit and cotton buds
- [ ] *Optional:* decorative trim or eyelets and multi-purpose glue or eyelet pliers
- [ ] Three-core earthed cable (to your desired length)
- [ ] Wire strippers or craft knife
- [ ] Pendant lampholder
- [ ] Small flathead screwdriver
- [ ] Lightbulb

Step 1

Remove the lid of the tin from inside the lip of the top edge. Clean the tin and remove any labels and glue with label remover. Mark the centre of the tin's base then, proceeding very slowly, drill a 3½in (3.5cm) hole in the tin's base. Ideally you would have an extra pair of strong hands to help hold the tin while you drill.

Step 2

If you are not intending to use an LED bulb, you will need to use a ¼in (6mm) drill bit to drill holes roughly 1in (2.5cm) apart just inside the edge of the tin base – this allows extra ventilation for the heat from a standard bulb. Clean off any burrs around all your drilled holes with a needle file.

Step 3

Prepare your tin for painting. Line the inside with a plastic carrier bag, fixing its open top edge in position with several lengths of masking tape. Run the top edge of the tape just below the lip of the tin as evenly and neatly as you can. The bag and tape will mask the inside of the tin from paint. The inside of my tin was white. This, or a plain metal interior, will help to reflect the light once the lamp is assembled.

Step 4

Now paint the outside of the tin. When using spray paint, always work in a well-ventilated area and protect any surrounding areas with a dustsheet or old newspaper. Spray numerous thin layers of paint, allowing drying time in between (see page 123).

Step 5

Carefully peel away the masking tape from around the inside edge of the tin and pull out the plastic bag to reveal a clean interior to the tin. You can use a cotton bud and white spirit to carefully clean away any paint that may have leaked under the masking tape. If you are planning to add trims, do this now, using either multi-purpose glue or decorative eyelets around the inside open edge of the tin (see Using Eyelet Pliers, page 122).

Step 6

Use a small strip of masking tape to prevent the fabric cord cover from fraying. Use wire strippers or a craft knife to prepare the wires in your cable for fixing onto the lampholder.

Step 7

Fit the lampholder following the manufacturer's instructions. Fit the other end of the cable to the ceiling rose, having firstly taken a bit of time to ascertain the height you want it to hang (this ought to be a job for a qualified electrician). Insert a lightbulb.

TIP

USING AN LED BULB REDUCES THE
HEAT AND ALLOWS YOU TO MAKE USE
OF SMALLER TIN CANS FOR PENDANT
LIGHT SHADES – ASK FOR ADVICE
FROM A QUALIFIED ELECTRICIAN.

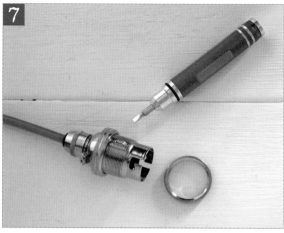

These sweet traditional brioche tins make perfect candle containers and look very pretty dotted around the home or as a table centrepiece. Add mosquito-repelling citronella oil for balmy alfresco summer nights or vanilla oil for the hint of freshly baked brioches.

BRIOCHE-TIN CANDLES

Supplies: *(makes three candles)*

- ☐ 3 x 4in (10cm) pre-waxed wick assembly
- ☐ 3 x small brioche tins or metal jelly moulds – roughly 5fl oz (150ml) capacity
- ☐ Glue dots or glue gun
- ☐ 6 x wick-supporting sticks (or wooden cooking skewers cut in half)
- ☐ 27oz (750g) of flaked soy wax – about 7½oz (225g) (or roughly twice the volume of your tin) for each candle

- ☐ 6 x small elastic bands
- ☐ Small pan or metal mixing bowl
- ☐ Large saucepan
- ☐ *Optional:* fragrance oil
- ☐ Old spoon
- ☐ Scissors

> **CANDLE SAFETY**
> Never leave a burning candle unattended.
> Keep them safely out of the reach of children,
> soft furnishings and flammable materials.

TIP

YOU CAN BUY COLOUR WAX FLAKES
OR ADD DYES TO YOUR WAX TO
COLOUR YOUR CANDLES.

Step 1
Fix the wick assembly to the centre of the bottom of your tins by using a glue dot or a dab of hot glue from a glue gun.

Step 2
Take the supporting sticks or skewers in pairs and hold them together by wrapping a small elastic band around them at either end. Use the skewers to hold the wicks vertically by resting them across the rim of each tin, the wicks pinched firmly between the skewers.

Step 3
Put the wax in a small pan or bowl and set the bowl in a pan of water on the hob over a medium heat. Add about three drops of fragrance oil (if using) to the wax. When melted, the wax will appear completely clear. Use your spoon to stir the oil into the wax.

Step 4
Pour a small amount of the liquid wax into the bottom of your prepared tins to just cover the metal wick assembly in each one. Leave to harden for about ten minutes. This is to make sure that the wicks stay in place for the main pour at Step 5.

Step 5
Return the pan to the hob to ensure the wax is fully melted, then pour it into your tins to within about ¼in (6mm) of the top edges and leave to cool and harden fully.

Step 6
Using scissors, trim the wicks to about ½in (12mm) from the top surface of the wax. Leave your candles for at least 24 hours before lighting.

TIP

IF THE WAX DRIES WITH A SMALL DIP
AROUND THE WICK, TOP IT UP WITH
MORE MELTED WAX, ENOUGH TO FILL
THE DIP AND THINLY COVER THE
SURFACE OF THE CANDLE EVENLY.

DECORATIONS

A beautiful decoration for inside or outside, this all-weather, all-season wreath is made from household wire and aluminium drinks cans. Use the printed colours and patterns already on the cans, or spray your blossoms to co-ordinate with your other decorations.

BLOSSOM WREATH

Supplies: *(makes a wreath roughly 16in [40cm] in diameter)*

- ☐ Tracing paper and pencil
- ☐ Heavy card
- ☐ Scissors
- ☐ Bradawl or small knitting needle
- ☐ 20 x 12fl oz (330ml) drinks cans (cut two blossoms from each can)
- ☐ Metal snips
- ☐ Old scissors
- ☐ *Optional:* protective gloves
- ☐ Wooden rolling pin
- ☐ Marker pen
- ☐ Bone folder or short knitting needle
- ☐ Ruler

- ☐ 8yd (7m) of 0.71mm (SWG 22, AWG 21) gauge wire
- ☐ Wire cutters
- ☐ Multi-purpose glue or glue gun
- ☐ Round-nose and flat-nose pliers
- ☐ 11yd (10m) of 1.25mm gauge wire

For the frame:

- ☐ 24 x 24in (60 x 60cm) MDF or plywood
- ☐ Hammer and 1¼in (3cm) panel pins
- ☐ String

Step 1

Cut out the blossom templates from page 130 in a heavy card. Use a bradawl or small knitting needle to pierce a hole in the centre of the templates as indicated.

Step 2

Rinse out a drinks can and shake it a few times to get rid of as much water as you can. Use metal snips to remove the top of the can.

Step 3

Using old scissors, cut down the side of the can from the top to the bottom, then cut off the bottom so that you are left with a rough rectangle of aluminium. Trim the edges with the scissors to remove any sharp bits and burrs. Strangely, this aluminium is not sharp once cut on the curve, but rough edges and sharp corners can be fierce, so you may want to wear protective gloves.

Step 4

At this point you can flatten the metal piece by rolling it back on its existing curvature – use a wooden rolling pin – but it's not necessary as, once you cut, score and fold your blossoms, they hold their own shape. Place a template down at one end of the rectangle and draw around it with a marker pen. Alternatively, you can score the aluminium with the pointed end of a bone folder (or knitting needle). Remember to mark the centre of the template, too.

Step 5

Remove the template and cut around the lines/scores using old scissors. Always cut into the points between the petals from either side.

Step 6

Using a ruler and bone folder, score along the front and back of the blossom, as indicated on the templates.

Step 7

Turn your work over and, again using a ruler and bone folder, crease along the shorter folds to make a three-dimensional decoration.

Step 8

Use the edge of the ruler or bone folder to crease along the long centres of each petal to the centre point, creasing from the other side along the shorter scores between the petals. Repeat Steps 2–7 until you have 40–50 blossoms in all (I made 20 large and 26 small ones for this wreath).

TIP

MAKE A HOLE WITH A KNITTING NEEDLE OR A BRADAWL AT THE TIP OF ONE PETAL AND THREAD 8IN (20CM) OF SILVER THREAD THROUGH IT TO TURN ONE OF THE BLOSSOMS INTO A HANGING DECORATION – THEY ARE WONDERFULLY LIGHT AND WILL TWIST AND FLUTTER IN THE SLIGHTEST OF BREEZES.

Step 9

Use a bradawl or a knitting needle to make a small hole through the centre of your flower.

Step 10

Cut a 4in (10cm) length of thin wire and use round-nose pliers to twist a small double loop at one end.

Step 11

Push the wire through the hole you pierced in the centre of the blossom from the front. Apply a spot of glue at the centre of the flower and pull the wire through so that the small coil stops at the hole and is anchored in the blob of glue. Leave to one side to dry fully. Do this with all the blossoms.

Step 12

Make the frame of the wreath by twisting and wrapping the heavier gauged wire into a circle. You can make a very simple jig for this: draw two concentric circles, the inner one 11in (28cm) in diameter and the outer one 15in (39cm) in diameter, on a piece of board. Now hammer 2in (5cm) panel pins in at random, about 3½in (9cm) apart along the outer circle and 3in (7.5cm) apart along the inner circle. Wrap the wire around the outside and inside circles before zigzagging it around from the outer nails to the inner nails.

Step 13

Make another couple of circuits around the jig, wrapping the wire at random angles and configurations around the nails. When you are happy with the structure, cut the wire and finish the final end off with a twist using flat-nose pliers.

Step 14

Cut short pieces of string and tie the wires together where they cross to retain the structure of the wire frame before you remove it from the nails of the jig.

Step 15

Remove one bit of string at a time and use your pliers and small lengths of the finer wire to replace them. Hold the wires firmly where they cross and bind them by winding the wire around tightly and cutting close with wire cutters.

Step 16

Working with one blossom at a time methodically from the back, cut the wire 'stems' to roughly 2in (5cm) and wrap them tightly around the base wires several times with flat-nose pliers before cutting the ends flush.

Step 17

Lay the completed wire frame in front of you and take your time arranging and then attaching your decorations – place the larger blossoms first, then fill in the gaps with smaller ones to ensure an even distribution across your wreath.

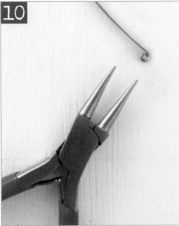

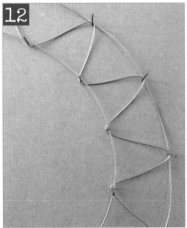

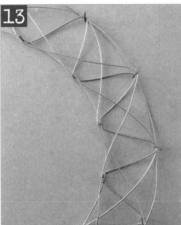

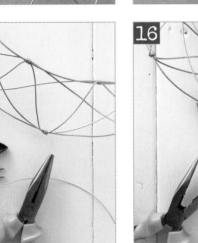

These decorations, reminiscent of little wind chimes, are a great project to make in just an hour or so. Use up precious, saved beads and wire to transform an old cookie cutter into a pretty, jangling ornament. Hang inside or outside to catch the breeze and light.

COOKIE-CUTTER CHIMES

Supplies: *(makes one decoration)*

- [ ] 3in (7.5cm) diameter cookie cutter (non-stainless steel, so it can be punched/drilled), with handle if possible
- [ ] Permanent marker pen
- [ ] Wooden log that fits snugly inside your cookie cutter (or a carpenter's vice)
- [ ] Hammer and large nail
- [ ] Drill and ⁵⁄₃₂in (4mm) drill bit
- [ ] Small needle file
- [ ] 12in (30cm) of 1.25mm galvanized wire
- [ ] Old wooden spoon, or ½in (12mm) diameter scrap of dowelling

- [ ] Wire cutters and flat-nosed pliers
- [ ] *Optional:* 1 aluminium drinks can (to make a handle if needed)
- [ ] Bone folder and ruler
- [ ] Multi-purpose glue
- [ ] String
- [ ] 39½in (1m) of 0.71mm (SWG 22, AWG 21) gauge galvanized wire
- [ ] Round-nose pliers
- [ ] ¼in (6mm) bells
- [ ] Small beads or bells (ensure the 0.71mm gauge wire fits through them)
- [ ] Old scissors

Step 1

Count the number of ridges around the cookie cutter and divide by seven – it may not fit exactly, but use the result to mark, with a permanent pen, seven points around the cutter at roughly equal intervals, and ⅜in (10mm) up from the bottom edge. Now slip the cutter over the end of the wooden log (or hold it firmly in a vice) and use a hammer and nail to punch dents at each of the seven marks – these will help prevent your drill from slipping. Use a drill to pierce seven holes around the edge of the cutter. You can pierce holes using a large nail and a hammer if you prefer, but this leaves a very rough hole and a lot of work for Step 2 (see page 122).

Step 2

Use a needle file to smooth off all the burrs and rough edges around each of the seven holes.

Step 3

Now make the jumprings. Take the heavier wire and wrap it evenly around the handle of a wooden spoon or a piece of dowelling. Slip the spring of wire off and cut along its length with wire cutters, through all the wraps, to leave you with a pile of rings.

Step 4

Pick the seven best rings and twist them slightly more open so that you can slip them through each of the seven holes. Use small flat-nose or round-nose pliers to tweak the rings back into perfect circles to secure them in place.

Step 5

Make a handle for your cutter if it doesn't have one. Cut a piece of aluminium from a drinks can following Steps 1–3 of the Blossom Wreath on page 74. Use a ruler and a bone folder to score lines on the printed side of the aluminium strip ½ x 6in (12 x 150mm) in from the two long edges. Fold these two edges in along the score lines and rub down gently – if you rub too firmly, you may split the fold.

Step 6

Use multi-purpose glue to attach the strip of aluminium to either side of the top edge of the cutter to make a curved handle: make sure that the folded side of the strip is underneath before following the manufacturer's instructions for gluing. Hold it in place with a piece of string before leaving it overnight to dry fully.

Step 7

Take four ¾in (2cm) lengths of the finer wire and use round-nose pliers to make a small loop at one end of it. Leave the loop slightly open.

Step 8

Thread a bell onto the loop and close it with round-nose pliers to hold it in place. Thread an assortment of beads onto the wire before using the pliers to create another little loop at the other end.

Step 9

Hook the beaded wire onto one of the jumprings, then use pliers to close it snugly before cutting the excess off with wire cutters. Repeat from Step 7 to complete your chime.

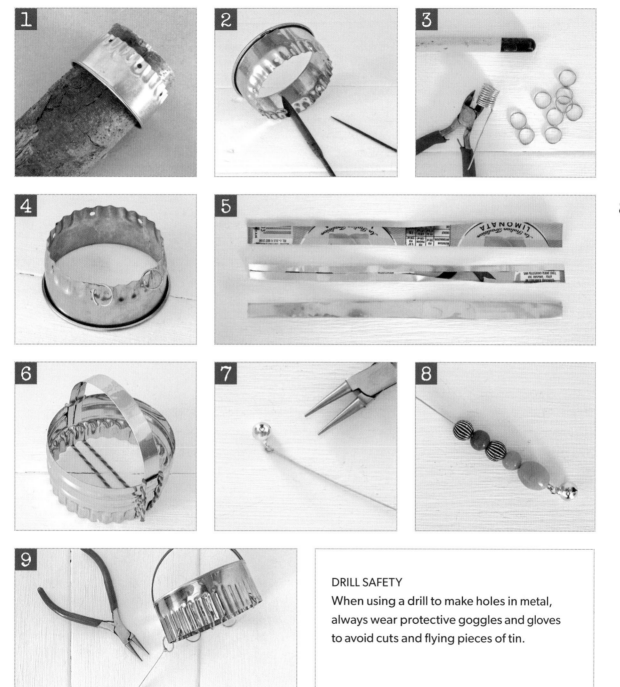

DRILL SAFETY
When using a drill to make holes in metal, always wear protective goggles and gloves to avoid cuts and flying pieces of tin.

This is a simple-looking frame for a favourite photograph. You need a bit more hardware to make it, but it's very satisfying to completely change the nature of a tin, not to mention the joy of hammering and making a noise! Rosettes add softness, and there is a nod to Regency-style architrave.

PICTURE FRAME

Supplies: *(makes one square frame)*

- ☐ 4 x tin cans of the same size (make sure they are the ones with ridges around them). The circumference will dictate the maximum length of the sides of your frame
- ☐ Can opener
- ☐ Label remover and soft, dry cloth
- ☐ Metal snips
- ☐ Protective gloves
- ☐ Hammer
- ☐ Metal try-square
- ☐ Vice

- ☐ Flat-nose pliers
- ☐ Permanent marker pen and ruler
- ☐ 1⅓in (4cm) diameter circular paper/card punch
- ☐ Bone folder or knitting needle
- ☐ 5/32in (4mm) eyelets
- ☐ Long-arm eyelet pliers
- ☐ Ring-pull drinks can
- ☐ Old scissors
- ☐ Multi-purpose glue
- ☐ *Optional:* Bulldog clips

Step 1

Use a can opener to remove the tops of the tins,
then clean the tins, using label remover if necessary.
Now use the can opener to take off the bottoms of
the tins. Be sure to do this from the side (see page
120) so there are no rims, otherwise you will not be
able to flatten your tin.

Cut down from the top to the bottom with tin snips
at 90 degrees and as neatly as you can. This will
leave very sharp edges, so wear protective gloves
when handling the cut tin. Finally, cut the flat top
and bottom strips off to within ⅜in (10mm) of either
side of the central ribbed area.

Step 2

You now need to flatten the rectangle of ribbed
tin into a flat(ish) sheet. Still wearing protective
gloves, pull the short ends apart gently to get
started. Then, using a hammer, start at one end
using the edge of your workbench, hammering
across the width of the tin an inch or two at a time.
The stiff ribs can take a good beating, but take it
slowly because deep creases won't come out.
The resulting sheet of metal will still be slightly
mottled and battered – full of character! Most of
any remaining curve in it will be evened out to
some extent when you fix the four sides of the
frame together.

Step 3

Fix a try-square firmly in a vice with the metal edge
up, parallel to your workbench.

Step 4

To finish off the two long edges, you need to fold
the flat areas over to the back of your work. Use
flat-nosed pliers to start this off ⅜in (10mm) in at
one end, along the edge of the first rib.

Step 5

Using the metal edge of your try-square and a
hammer, work on the length of the tin to fold it
back upon itself all the way along.

Step 6

Repeat Step 5 with the other long end of the sheet
of tin. Lay your work right side up and flat on the
workbench. Hammer methodically all along both
folded edges to make them even and neat.

Step 7

Turn the sheet of metal over – now wrong side up.
Mark a line with a permanent pen and a ruler ¼in
(6mm) from one end.

Step 8

Use the flat-nose pliers to fold the ¼in (6mm) edge
towards the back of your work, leaving it at a right
angle (90 degrees). Repeat Steps 1–8 with the
remaining three tin cans.

Step 9

For the rosettes, open out the drinks can following
Steps 2–3 of the Blossom Wreath on page 74. Use
the circular punch to cut out four perfect circles.
Keep the scraps for Step 12.

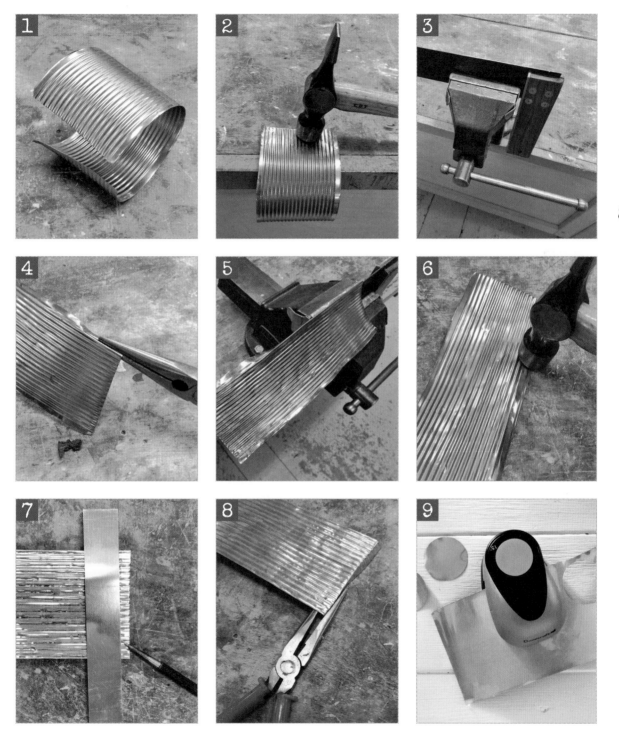

Step 10

Take one circle of aluminium. Use a ruler and a bone folder, or the tip of a knitting needle, to score lines across the centre of the circle four times to divide it into roughly equal eighths.

Step 11

Turn the circle over and score another four lines across it, each one between the lines scored on the other side. You now have a circle marked into sixteenths with the lines scored on alternate sides of the metal circle. Use the edge of your bone folder or knitting needle to fold the creases on alternate sides to give you a crimped, stylized rosette. Use long-arm eyelet pliers to punch a $5/32$in (4mm) hole in the centre of your rosette.

Step 12

To make the corners for holding your photograph to the back of the frame, use scraps of aluminium from the drinks can and, using old scissors, cut four right-angled triangles using the template on page 132.

Step 13

Score $5/32$in (4mm) in along all three edges and fold over. Rub the folds down with a bone folder or your thumbnail **13a** . Snip the corners off with the old scissors **13b**.

Step 14

Decide on the dimensions of your frame at this point. For a square frame, measure the sheets of tin and trim all the unfolded ends of them to match the length of the shortest. If you want a rectangular frame, cut the unfolded end of two sheets shorter. Now assemble the frame by fixing the corners. Lay the tin pieces out upside down, following the layout template on page 132. Working on one corner at a time, lay one sheet in front of you with its folded end on the right. Lay the next sheet vertically on top of the right-hand end with the bottom edges aligning and its unfolded end tucked snugly into the angle of the folded end beneath. Use a hammer to fold the right-hand edge over completely to hold the two pieces together, ensuring they are snugly together. You can apply multi-purpose glue between the layers of metal at this stage. If you do, follow the manufacturer's instructions and use bulldog clips to hold the layers together at each corner. Leave to dry overnight.

Step 15

Finish each corner off by using an eyelet to join a triangle of aluminium on the back (to hold a photo) and a rosette on the front. With the frame wrong side up, use a permanent marker to draw a line at each corner from the outside point to the inside edge. Mark a point 1in (2.5cm) along this line from the inside edge of the frame and punch a $5/32$in (4mm) hole through both layers of tin with the eyelet pliers **15a**. Place a rosette in the first corner, pushing an eyelet through the centre hole, and through the frame's double layer of metal **15b**.

Step 16

Push a triangle of aluminium onto the back of the eyelet before fixing it using the long-arm eyelet pliers. In doing this you will sandwich the double layer of metal between a rosette on the front and a triangle at the back. The elements will be in the following order in the eyelet pliers: eyelet, rosette, frame, triangle. Squeeze the pliers firmly to ensure everything is fixed securely. Place a photograph into the back of the frame, tucking the corners into the aluminium triangles to hold it in place.

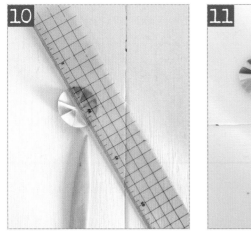

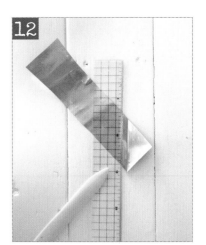

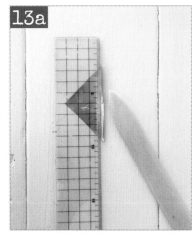

These bright and festive discs can be used to celebrate any special occasion. String them along to make a garland or hang a single disc in a window to catch the breeze and spin. Use pastels for Easter, bright and zingy colours in summer, darker colours for autumn and winter.

DISC DECORATIONS

Supplies: *(makes one decoration)*

- [ ] Tin can
- [ ] Can opener
- [ ] Label remover and soft, dry cloth
- [ ] Hammer
- [ ] Needle file
- [ ] Photocopier, or a sheet of tracing paper and copier paper
- [ ] Paper and pencil
- [ ] Compass
- [ ] Permanent marker pen
- [ ] ⁵⁄₃₂in (4mm) long-arm hole punch or drill and ⁵⁄₃₂in (4mm) drill bit

- [ ] Spray paint or enamel/metal paint and paintbrush
- [ ] 9 x colour ⁵⁄₃₂in (4mm) eyelets and eyelet pliers*
- [ ] 2mm (UK14:USB/1) crochet hook
- [ ] Scraps of 4-ply cotton yarn or cotton embroidery thread
- [ ] Scissors

* *You may need long-arm pliers to reach to the middle of your disc*

Step 1

Cut your tin using a can opener on the side of it so that no sharp edges are left on the lid you will be using (see page 120). Clean the tin and remove any labels or glue using label remover. Use a hammer to tap all around the under-edge or run a flat needle file around it; this will dull any sharp residue from the cutting.

Step 2

Make a template for your discs (see page 130). Cut the template out around the outer (black) line. Fold it in half and lay on top of the disc. Use a permanent marker pen to mark a dot at the centre of your disc, indicated by the red dot.

Step 3

Cut along the innner (blue) circle. Centre the template on your disc and use your pen to mark eight points around your disc at the position of each black dot.

Step 4

Use a punch – or a drill and drill bit – to make ⁵⁄₃₂in (4mm) holes at each of the marked points and one where you have marked the centre of the lid (see page 122).

Step 5

Now spray or hand-paint both sides of the discs (see page 123). Don't worry about the rough edges you may have around the holes, as these will be covered by the eyelets later.

Step 6

One at a time, insert an eyelet into the punched holes and fix them firmly with either pliers or the gadget supplied by the manufacturer.

Step 7

Use a crochet hook and cotton yarn to decorate the outside edge of your disc – add three double crochet stitches through each eyelet and three or four chain stitches in between them, depending on your tension and the circumference of your lid. You want the edge of the lid to be covered snugly by the crocheted cotton.

Make a slipknot 8in (20cm) from the end of your yarn. With the front of the disc facing you, push your hook through an eyelet and wrap the yarn around it. Pull a loop through to the front, then wrap the yarn over the hook again.

Pull the wrapped yarn through both loops, with one loop remaining on the hook.

This completes one double crochet stitch. Make one more dc into the same eyelet.

*3 ch, 3 dc into next eyelet, repeat from * until you have worked all 8 eyelets. 3 ch, 1 dc into first eyelet, sl st into top of your first dc.

Cut the tail end to 8in (20cm). Pull the tail of yarn through the loop on your hook.

Step 8

Tie the two tails together with a knot about 1in (2.5cm) from their ends and trim both ends to ³⁄₈in (10mm) – this creates a hanging loop for your decoration.

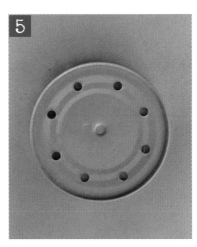

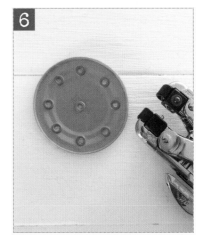

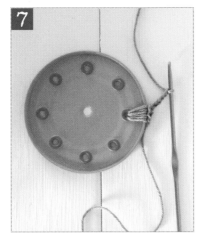

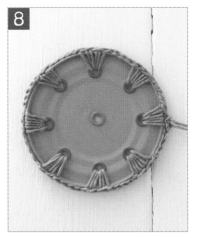

TIP

FOR A QUICK PROJECT,
LEAVE OUT THE SPRAY
PAINTING AT STEP 6 AND
THE CROCHETED EDGE AT
STEP 8 AND SIMPLY USE
A LENGTH OF STRING TO
MAKE A HANGING LOOP.

GIFTS

Give someone the gift of a tiny allotment! In just a few days, they will be able to grow fresh cress to add to salads and sandwiches. There are enough seeds to keep sowing and harvesting. Make a matching tin of mustard seeds, too, or include a recipe for luxurious quail's egg sandwiches.

CRESS-GROWING KIT

Supplies:

- [ ] Lidded tin – this one measures 4 x 3 x 1½in (10 x 8 x 4cm)
- [ ] Dustsheet or newspaper
- [ ] Spray paint – light and dark green
- [ ] Masking tape
- [ ] Scalpel
- [ ] Steel ruler
- [ ] Cutting mat
- [ ] *Optional:* Bone folder
- [ ] Fine paintbrush

- [ ] White and green acrylic paints
- [ ] Photocopier
- [ ] A4 paper
- [ ] Spray or multi-purpose glue
- [ ] Soft cloth
- [ ] Scissors
- [ ] 2 tsp cress seeds
- [ ] Glue stick
- [ ] Cotton wool

Step 1

Protect the area around your tin lid with newspaper or a dustsheet and, following the manufacturer's instructions, spray paint (see page 123) the outside of the lid with several thin layers of colour. Leave to dry fully. When dry, you can do the same with another colour on the inside of the lid if you wish – it's wise to use masking tape to prevent the paint straying onto the outside of the lid.

Step 2

Use a scalpel, steel ruler and a cutting mat to cut ten very fine strips of masking tape – 1/16 x 1¾in (2mm x 3.5cm). With your lid right side up and laid out in a landscape position, arrange the strips randomly across the lid to create the stalks of your illustrated cress, as shown below. Using a bone folder or a fingernail, rub the thin strips of tape down carefully to ensure they are firmly stuck down.

Step 3

Using a fine paintbrush and the illustration below as a guide, paint simple, stylized leaves at the top of your masking-tape stalks. Mix the two colours of acrylic paint in different quantities to make an array of hues of green. These will dry fairly rapidly – just wait a few minutes and add a second layer of paint to ensure a good, flat colour on each leaf.

Step 4

If you want to include the quail's egg and cress sandwich recipe on page 133, it's really cute to stick an image of a beautiful, speckled egg on the inside of the lid (take your own photo or copy the one on page 133). Use spray or multi-purpose glue to stick your chosen egg image carefully to the centre of the lid. Use a soft cloth to ensure the picture is fully adhered to the surface.

Step 5

Photocopy the cress-growing instructions and envelope template from page 133, re-sizing the seed envelope template if necessary so that the central panel fits comfortably within your tin. Cut out and score along the dotted lines using a bone folder or the handle end of your scalpel along the edge of the steel ruler.

Step 6

Fold along the scored lines and glue where indicated to make your seed envelope. Photocopy the recipe from page 133, if you are including it, and cut it down to fit the envelope. Add a couple of teaspoons of cress seeds to the envelope and seal it with a glue stick. Cut a piece of cotton wool to fit the inside of your tin. Put it in the tin base and place the seed envelope on top of it before pushing the lid on snugly to finish the project.

A memory tin is a great way to store precious memories of holidays and other special events – not just photographs, tickets and postcards, but little beach finds and even pressed flowers and leaves – all kept safe in a handmade 'envelope book' that sits inside the tin.

MEMORY TIN

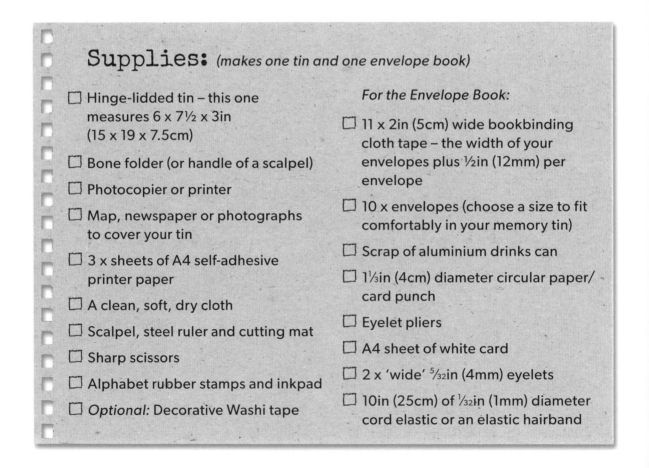

Supplies: *(makes one tin and one envelope book)*

- [ ] Hinge-lidded tin – this one measures 6 x 7½ x 3in (15 x 19 x 7.5cm)
- [ ] Bone folder (or handle of a scalpel)
- [ ] Photocopier or printer
- [ ] Map, newspaper or photographs to cover your tin
- [ ] 3 x sheets of A4 self-adhesive printer paper
- [ ] A clean, soft, dry cloth
- [ ] Scalpel, steel ruler and cutting mat
- [ ] Sharp scissors
- [ ] Alphabet rubber stamps and inkpad
- [ ] *Optional:* Decorative Washi tape

For the Envelope Book:

- [ ] 11 x 2in (5cm) wide bookbinding cloth tape – the width of your envelopes plus ½in (12mm) per envelope
- [ ] 10 x envelopes (choose a size to fit comfortably in your memory tin)
- [ ] Scrap of aluminium drinks can
- [ ] 1⅓in (4cm) diameter circular paper/card punch
- [ ] Eyelet pliers
- [ ] A4 sheet of white card
- [ ] 2 x 'wide' 5⁄32in (4mm) eyelets
- [ ] 10in (25cm) of 1⁄32in (1mm) diameter cord elastic or an elastic hairband

Step 1

Remove the lid from your tin if possible – this can be done by using a bone folder to ease the hinges open from the inside of the base of the tin.

Step 2

Photocopy/print your map, photographs or newspaper cuttings in colour (or black and white if you wish) onto an A4 sheet of self-adhesive printing paper. Make another copy to cover the sides, and a third if you want to line the inside of your lid – a laser printer is best for this, as other printers can run and smudge if splashed with water or other fluids.

Step 3

Place the lid top up on a flat surface. Lay the copied map, centred, on top of it, right side up and with plenty of overlap around all sides. Peel away the backing paper from, initially, about ⅜in (10mm) of the left-hand edge of the paper before steadily pulling the rest of the backing paper away to the right and leaving the printed map covering the lid. Use a soft, dry cloth to smooth any air bubbles caught beneath the paper to the edges to ensure the photograph is fully adhered to the tin surface. Repeated rubbing and smoothing is worth it for consistent and permanent adhesion.

Step 4

Use your bone folder (or a thumbnail) to ensure firm adhesion along any ridges around the top perimeter of the lid. Rub one edge down along one side of the lid. Use your bone folder (or a thumbnail) to push the paper into the rim/lip of the edge of the lid to create a crease.

Step 5

Gently pull the adhesive paper away from the tin and run a sharp scalpel along this crease.

Step 6

Remove the excess and smooth the paper back along the rimmed edge and into the rim with a bone folder or fingernail to remove any air bubbles. Repeat this process with the remaining three edges, leaving spare paper at all four corners. Use sharp scissors to snip three or four angled cuts into each corner.

TIP

YOU CAN USE SPRAY GLUE TO STICK DOWN AN ORIGINAL MAP. REMEMBER TO WORK IN A WELL-VENTILATED SPACE OR, PREFERABLY, OUTSIDE. IT'S BEST TO USE RE-POSITIONABLE SPRAY GLUE, JUST IN CASE YOU MISJUDGE IT FIRST TIME ROUND.

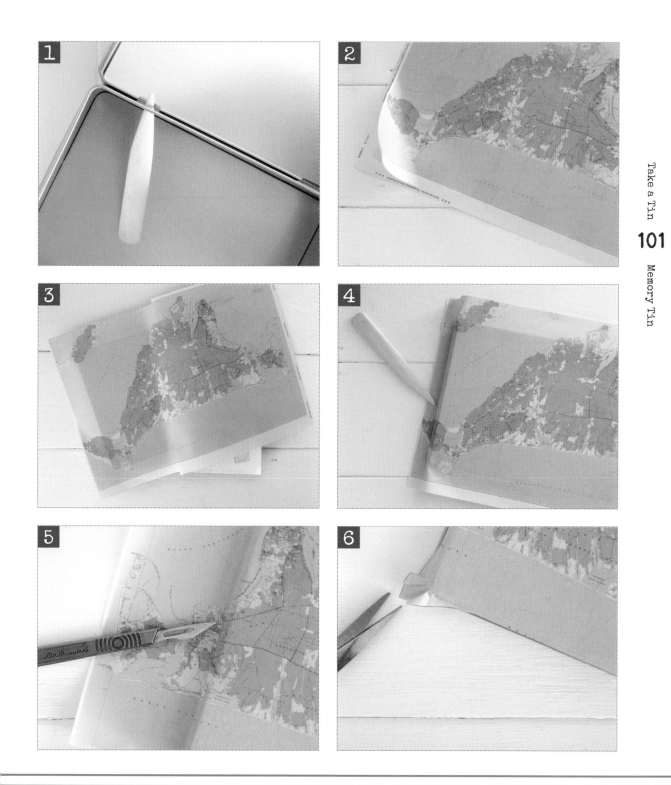

Step 7

Overlap and rub down the angled corner strips to create as smooth a corner as you can. Finally, run a scalpel along the contour of the rim at the corners and remove the excess paper scraps. Once again, rub down firmly with a bone folder or fingernail to leave clean, curved edges.

Step 8

Use your scalpel to cut slits in the hinge holes from the inside of the lid before reattaching the lid, using the bone folder to close the hinges again.

Step 9

Make more copies of your map and cover the sides of the tin. Keep any joins and overlaps away from the front and preferably towards the back of the two sides. Overlap the paper by about ⅜in (10mm) rather than attempting a flush join of two edges butting together. Finish the paper short of the top edge, whether there is a lip (as on my tin here) or not; the extra bulk of paper will make the lid fit more tightly and the paper could tear and buckle. On some tins, the lid may be fairly loose, in which case overlap the paper by about ⅜in (10mm) and fold and stick it over the top lip and into the inside of the tin (see the Magnetic Pinboard project, Steps 2–4, page 34).

Step 10

You can line the inside of the lid with another map, photograph or postcard. To make a snug-fitting template, follow the instructions for the Box Pincushion project, Steps 12–13, page 42.

Step 11

Use your alphabet stamps to print a date or name on a scrap of thick card before cutting it out neatly using a scalpel and ruler.

Step 12

Use decorative Washi tape or glue to affix the printed label onto the lid of the box. If using tape, trim it neatly and give it a good rub all the way around with a fingernail or bone folder to make sure it is fully adhered and there are no creases or air bubbles.

TIP

GIVE THE OUTSIDE OF YOUR TIN A COUPLE OF THIN COATS OF MATT VARNISH TO MAKE IT MORE HARD-WEARING.

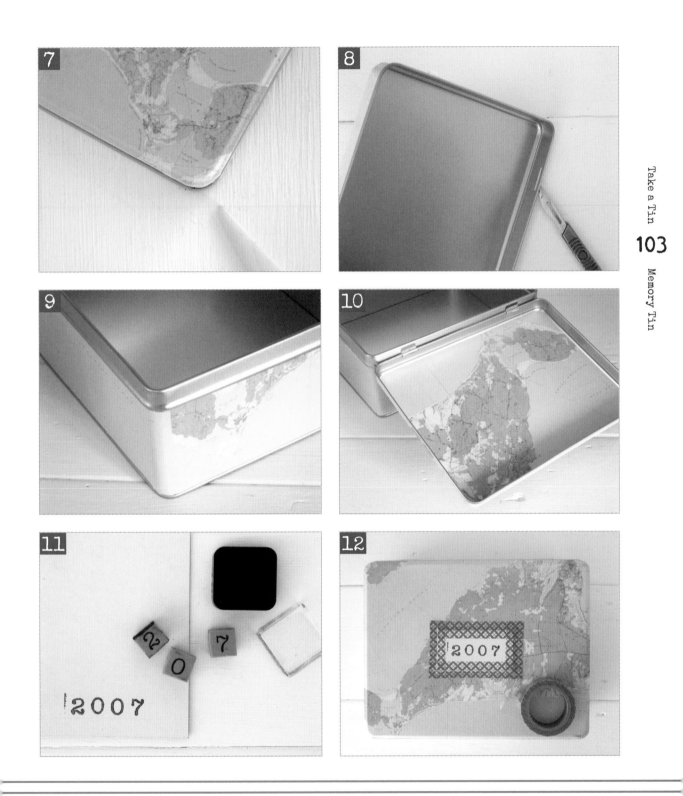

ENVELOPE BOOK

Keep tickets, leaves, photographs, postcards and other special holiday finds in a handmade book of envelopes. You can make your book as thick as you like, using tape, elastic and a small circle from an aluminium drinks can to add a little colour.

Step 1

Cut one piece of book binding the width of an envelope plus ½in (12mm). Lay it down horizontally in front of you and lay an envelope on top of this, flap side up and furthest from you, so that the bottom edge lies along the centre of the tape, leaving the top 1in (2.5cm) of the tape covered. You should have a small overhang of tape on either side. Holding the envelope down firmly in position, carefully pull away the backing from the fabric tape.

Step 2

Use your fingers to rub along the bottom of the envelope to ensure it is firmly adhered to the tape. Take a second envelope, flap side down and nearest you, and butt the top edge of it snugly against the bottom of the first envelope. Rub along the top edge of the second envelope, again to ensure it is firmly adhered.

Step 3

Fold the bottom envelope up to cover the top envelope perfectly and rub along the bottom edge of the now folded tape.

Step 4

Repeat steps 1–3 until you have used all ten envelopes.

Step 5

Trim the overhanging ends of tape on both sides of your book – doing these one at a time is neater.

Step 6

If your envelopes are self adhesive, work through your book one at a time peeling off the backing tape and covering the sticky strip with decorative Washi tape, cutting it flush with the edge of the envelope flap on either side. You can decorate the front envelope of the book with another strip of tape along the front edge of the flap, trimmed flush at either side with scissors.

Step 7

To make a sleeve for the book, first punch a circle of aluminium from the drinks can, following the instructions in Step 9 of the Picture Frame project on page 84). Punch a ⁵⁄₃₂in (4mm) hole in the centre of it with eyelet pliers. Cut a strip of card from the A4 sheet along its length, roughly 12 x 2½in (30 x 6cm). Wrap it around your book and cut it to adjust the length so that the two ends just slightly overlap by 1in (2.5cm). Mark two points, each one centrally along the length and 1¾in (4.5cm) from one end and 1in (2.5cm) from the other. Punch a ⁵⁄₃₂in (4mm) hole at each marked point. Fix a 'wide' eyelet, attaching your punched aluminium circle through the first hole and simply a 'wide' eyelet in the second. Fold the piece of elastic in half and tie a double knot near the raw ends.

Step 8

To wrap your book, push the looped end of the elastic through the plain eyelet from the back to the front and secure it around the aluminium disc.

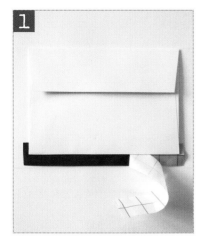

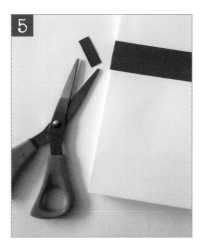

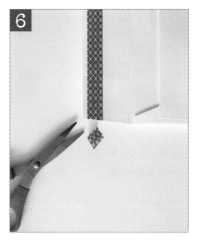

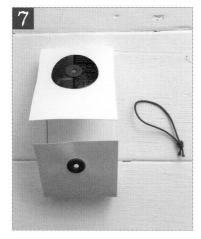

TIP

EXPERIMENT BY USING
COLOURED ENVELOPES,
OR EVEN MAKE YOUR
OWN OUT OF OLD MAPS.

This is a cute bracelet, upcycled from old ring-pulls. Once you've mastered the technique, you can play around using various colour cords and ring-pulls, even incorporating beads. Before long, you'll find yourself diving into the recycling to retrieve tiny bits of tin treasure.

RING-PULL BRACELET

Supplies: *(makes one bracelet approximately 8½in (22cm) in diameter, using ring-pulls roughly ⅝in (15mm) in width and 1in (2.5cm) in length, although you can make this project any size you like)*

- [ ] 21 ring-pulls – preferably all of the same shape and size
- [ ] Small wire snips
- [ ] Flat needle file
- [ ] 3 x 18in (45cm) lengths of different-coloured cotton cord approximately ⅟₃₂in (1mm) thick

- [ ] 8 x silver ⅛ x ⅛in (3 x 3mm) crimp tubes
- [ ] Flat-nose pliers
- [ ] Small crochet hook
- [ ] ⅜in (10mm) diameter metal button
- [ ] Sharp scissors

Step 1

Prepare your ring-pulls. Remove the tab and any sharp bits of metal at the point where it was attached to the can. Snip these off with small wire snips and use a flat needle file to file off any sharp edges left.

Step 2

Thread all three lengths of cotton cord through one of the crimp tubes and use flat-nosed pliers to squeeze it flat 1in (2.5cm) from the central point of the cords. If you are using different coloured cords, make sure that at the point of crimping they are laid in the order you want them. I used dark pink, medium pink and light pink.

Step 3

Take the longer side of the cords and braid them together tightly for 2in (5cm). Thread on a second crimp tube and, again making sure the cords are in the correct order if you are using different colours, use the flat-nose pliers to flatten the tube and grip them firmly in place.

Step 4

Bend your lengths of cord exactly in half. Your two crimp tubes will now lie next to each other, a braided loop above them and the six cords lying in a row together below them. The colours for mine were as follows: cords 1 and 6, dark pink; cords 2 and 5, medium pink; cords 3 and 4, light pink. Take the two central cords (cords 3 and 4), feed them through a third crimp tube, pushing it snugly up against the other two flattened tubes. Making sure they are not twisted nor overlapping, flatten the tube firmly with the pliers.

TIP

LAY OUT YOUR RING-PULLS BEFORE STARTING STEP 5. IF SOME ARE DIFFERENT COLOURS, TAKE CARE ARRANGING THEIR POSITION IN YOUR DESIGN.

Step 5

Working from left to right – and with the braided loop on your left – place your first ring-pull on top of the threads. Using a small crochet hook, pull the top three cords through the top hole of the ring-pull from the back to the front, and the bottom three cords through the bottom one, again from the back to the front.

Step 6

Lay the second ring-pull on top of the first, covering the right-hand side of it. Insert the crochet hook from the back to the front, up through the top hole of the first and the second ring-pulls. Use the hook to pull the top three cords through the top hole of both rings to the back of your work. Do the same with the bottom three cords and the bottom holes.

TIP

IF YOU LAY THE RING-PULLS OUT WITH 11 BUTTED UP IN A ROW NEXT TO EACH OTHER, THEN 10 ON TOP OF THESE, THE LENGTH OF THIS, PLUS 1¾IN (4.5CM), WILL GIVE YOU THE FINAL LENGTH OF YOUR BRACELET.

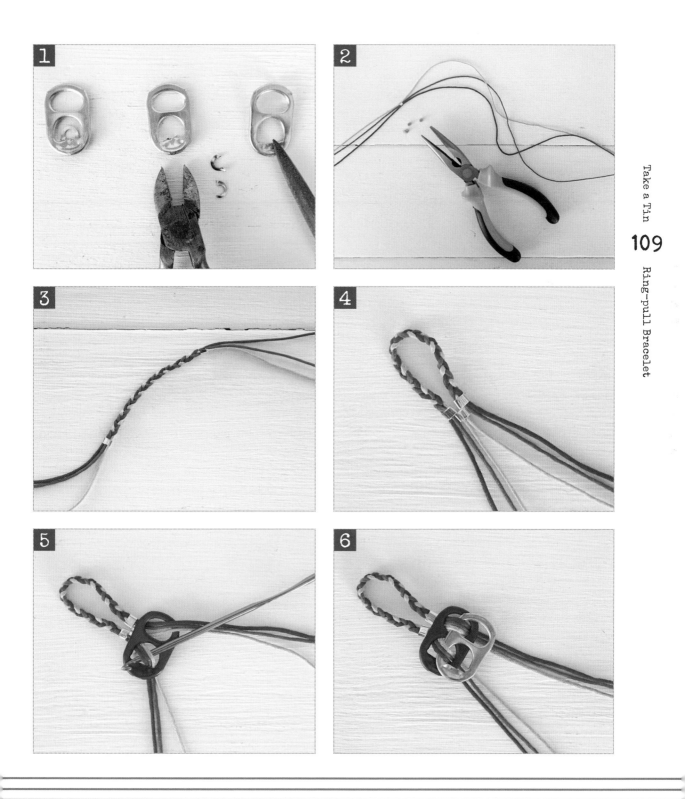

Step 7

Take a third ring-pull and place it under the right-hand side of the second one, butting up to the right-hand edge of the first one. Insert the crochet hook from the front to the back, down through the top hole of the second and third ring-pulls. Use the hook to pull the top three cords up through the top hole of both rings to the front of your work. Do the same with the bottom three cords and the bottom holes.

Step 8

Repeat Step 5. Position the fourth ring-pull on top of the third one, covering the right-hand side of it, butting up to the right-hand edge of the second one. Insert the crochet hook from the back to the front, up through the top hole of the first and the second ring-pulls. Use the hook to pull the top three cords through the top hole of both rings to the back of your work. Do the same with the bottom three cords and the bottom holes.

Step 9

When you have joined on your last ring-pull, insert the hook through its top hole from the back to the front and pull the top three cords through to the back. Do the same with the bottom three cords through the bottom hole. Turn your work over and thread a crimp tube on to the two middle cords. Push it snugly down as far as it will go against the ring-pull and crimp it firmly with flat-nose pliers.

Step 10

Now thread another crimp tube along the top three cords, push it snugly against the first crimp tube and flatten it firmly. Do the same with the bottom three cords, too.

Step 11

Take the fourth cord from the top and thread it through from the back to the front of the button, then back again through the other hole from the front to the back. Now take a crimp tube and thread the cord through it. Fold the cord over so that it lies back across the ring-pulls. Feed the fifth and sixth cords through the same crimp tube from left to right, so that their tail ends lie away from the ring-pulls. With the fourth cord in your left hand and the fifth and sixth in your right hand, tug gently at them so that the button lies about ⅜in (10mm) from the last ring-pull. Crimp the tube with flat-nose pliers, ensuring that the three of them lie in the right order if you are using different colours.

Step 12

Repeat Step 11 with the third cord (light pink in this case) from the top, threading it through the same button, back through the crimping tube holding the first and second cords and fixing it firmly with the flat-nose pliers. Trim the cord ends to about ⅜in (10mm).

WHY NOT MAKE A
MATCHING NECKLACE
BY USING MORE
RING-PULLS AND
LARGER LENGTHS
OF COTTON CORD?

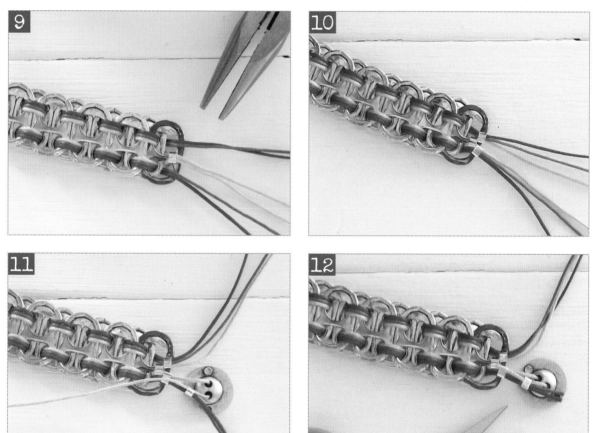

A quick and easy project to entertain every member of the family. Make your own magnetic travel games simply using pencil tins and homemade counters. They're slim enough to pop into your bag, ready for playing on train and car trips or when waiting in a restaurant.

TRAVEL GAMES

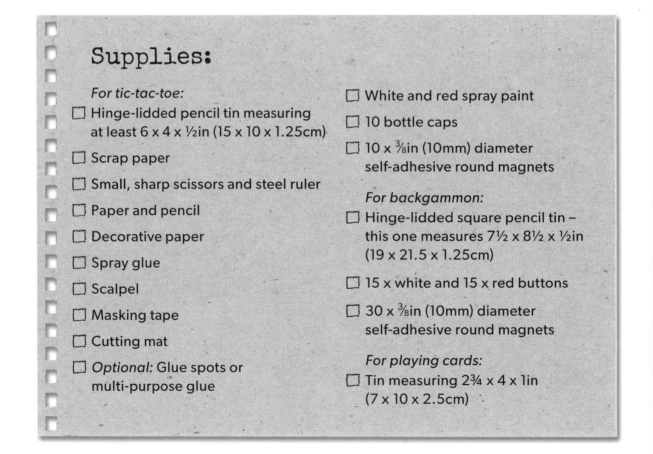

Supplies:

For tic-tac-toe:
- ☐ Hinge-lidded pencil tin measuring at least 6 x 4 x ½in (15 x 10 x 1.25cm)
- ☐ Scrap paper
- ☐ Small, sharp scissors and steel ruler
- ☐ Paper and pencil
- ☐ Decorative paper
- ☐ Spray glue
- ☐ Scalpel
- ☐ Masking tape
- ☐ Cutting mat
- ☐ *Optional:* Glue spots or multi-purpose glue

- ☐ White and red spray paint
- ☐ 10 bottle caps
- ☐ 10 x ⅜in (10mm) diameter self-adhesive round magnets

For backgammon:
- ☐ Hinge-lidded square pencil tin – this one measures 7½ x 8½ x ½in (19 x 21.5 x 1.25cm)
- ☐ 15 x white and 15 x red buttons
- ☐ 30 x ⅜in (10mm) diameter self-adhesive round magnets

For playing cards:
- ☐ Tin measuring 2¾ x 4 x 1in (7 x 10 x 2.5cm)

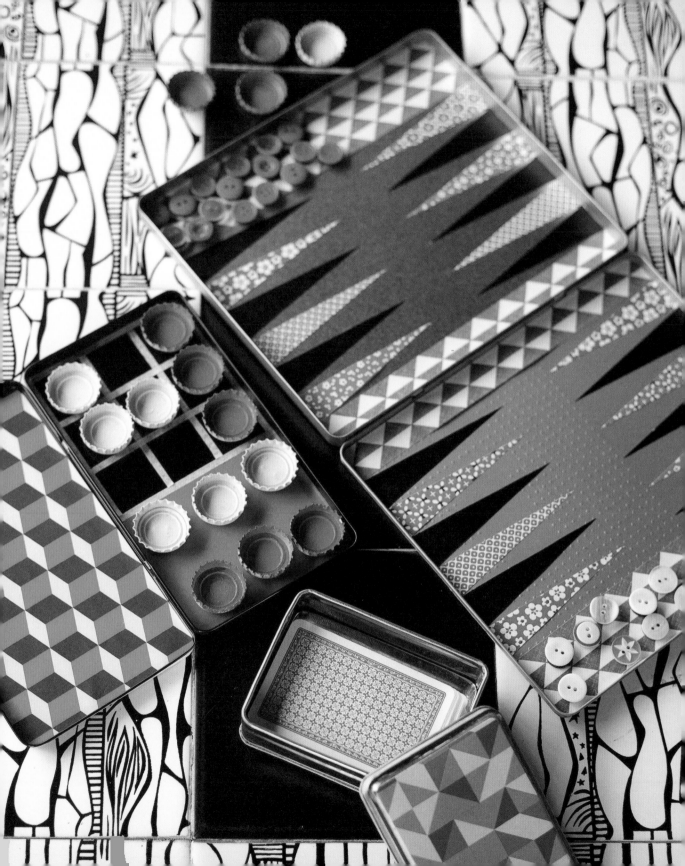

TIP

THE INSTRUCTIONS GIVEN HERE
ARE FOR TRAVEL TIC-TAC-TOE
BUT YOU COULD MAKE A BACKGAMMON
SET IN A SIMILAR WAY USING A
LARGER TIN AND THE TEMPLATE
ON PAGE 132.

Step 1

Remove the pencils and the moulded plastic tray from your hinged tin. Make a template of the lid of your tin by drawing around it on a scrap of paper. Cut out the paper template and fold it in half along both axes. Open it out and mark the two creases in pencil using a ruler.

Step 2

Cut out a piece of decorative paper, using the template as a guide. Use the pencil lines on your template to help you to centre it on the paper's pattern.

Step 3

Stick the decorative paper templates onto the lid of your tin using spray glue. Give it a good rub all over to make sure the paper is well stuck, right up to the edges. Then, using small, sharp scissors, trim any overhang of paper around the edge of the lid.

Step 4

Open up the tin and push the paper template into the lid. Use a bone folder or your thumbnail to press the paper into all the corners and edges. Take the template out again and cut along the new creases to make a new template, then cut out a piece of decorative paper from this new template to line the lid. The narrowest measurement of this template is measurement A. Cut another piece of paper to fit into the bottom of the tin. This one should be the same size minus measurement A. Stick this piece in on the left-hand side of the base using spray glue – it should leave you with a square area uncovered on the right for your tic-tac-toe grid. Glue the piece of paper in to line the lid.

Step 5

Using a scalpel and ruler, stick a strip of masking tape onto a cutting mat and slice it into $\frac{3}{16}$in (5mm) strips. Stick the strips down on the right-hand side of the bottom of your tin to form a nine-square grid. Use the scalpel to trim the strips neatly and rub them down firmly with your thumbnail or a bone folder to ensure firm contact along their lengths.

Step 6

Before spraying the insides of the bottle tops with white paint, use a small roll of masking tape, or a glue spot, on the bottom of each to prevent them from moving about while spraying. Spray paint a couple of extra ones, just to have spares. Spray half your lids with another coat of red paint.

Step 7

Once dried, remove any masking tape or glue dots from the backs of the bottle caps and stick a magnet to the centre back of each.

TIP

YOU COULD MAKE SMALLER
COUNTERS WITH BUTTONS RATHER
THAN THE BOTTLE CAPS.

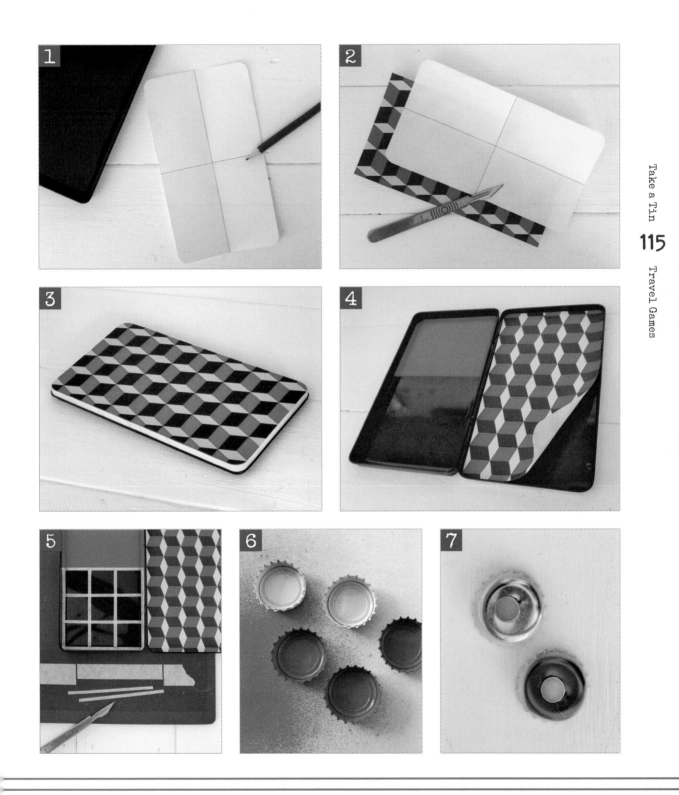

TECHNIQUES

MATERIALS AND EQUIPMENT

A drill and drill bits, as well as a sewing machine and access to a photocopier, would be useful for some projects in this book.

Other items you will need include:
Screws, nails and eyelets (1), wire cutters/strippers (2), drill bits (3), wire wool (4), eyelet pliers (5), paintbrushes (6), crochet hooks (7), metal paint (8), pliers – ideally flat-nose (9), round-nose (10) and long-nose (11), bradawl (12), hammer (13), spray paint (14), needle files (15), galvanized wire (16), tin snips (17), screwdriver (18), an assortment of tin cans (19), protective gloves and goggles (20), old scissors (21), can openers (22), long-arm eyelet pliers/punch (23), soy wax pellets (24), candle wicks (25), bone folder (26), scalpel (27), metal ruler (28), masking and Washi tapes (29).

> **TIN SAFETY**
> Metal is great for creating beautiful projects, but tin cans can be very sharp to work with.
> I recommend you read the information in this chapter and take the basic but important
> precautions outlined before starting on a project.

OPENING TIN CANS

There are two ways to open your food cans: through the top (the inside edge of the lid) or around the side (the outside edge of the lid). The can opener will usually leave one safe edge and one sharp edge after cutting.

If you plan to use the body of the can, open your tin around the inside edge of the lid. Hold the can upright on a solid surface, positioning the can opener so that the cutting wheel is over the lip of the edge and on the top surface of the can (**A**).

If you are going to use the lid or base of your can, open it around the outside edge of the lid. The small wheel of the can opener should be beneath the lip on the outside of the can (**B**).

Hold both handles of the can opener loosely in your hand. Squeeze the handles until you see the cutting wheel puncture the tin. Turn the hand key on the can opener clockwise while still squeezing the handles together firmly. When the cutter reaches the full circle it will cut the final piece with a snapping noise.

Open the handles of the can opener and detach it from the can. Remove the separated lid from the opened can, being careful of the very sharp edges.

CLEANING TIN CANS

Remove any paper labels and wash your tin thoroughly with hot soapy water – preferably in a dishwasher –being careful of your fingers with any sharp edges. After washing, you will most likely still have glue residue from any paper labels. This can be removed very efficiently with label-removing fluid. Apply the fluid using a cotton rag and rub until any glue has been removed. Always follow the instructions on the bottle and work in a well-ventilated area.

TOOLS FOR TIN CUTTING

SCISSORS (A)
An old pair of scissors is very efficient for cutting aluminium drinks cans, but make sure you don't use a good pair – it will not be the same again.

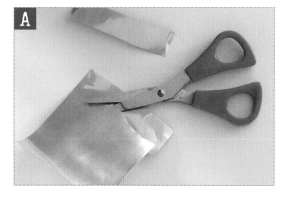

TIN SNIPS (B)
Cutting sheet metal with tin snips can be tricky and frustrating. The edges are sharp and the cutoffs are stiff and get caught in carpets and floorboards, so DO NOT walk about with bare feet! Ask for advice when buying tin or metal snips. The toughest metal you will tackle in this book is a standard tin can. Large snips can be a bit unwieldy to handle. One way to facilitate the use of tin snips is to clamp them in a vice and use just the free handle to cut with.

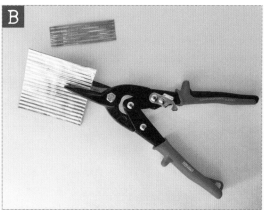

CUTTING SAFETY
Always protect your eyes when using tools to cut metal, and wear thick gloves when handling freshly cut, raw edges.

PUNCHING HOLES AND PAINTING TINS

MAKING HOLES WITH A NAIL OR PUNCH (A)

Use a heavy hammer and place something hard, ideally a piece of wood, between the metal and your work surface so the nail or punch doesn't damage it when it pierces the metal. Different-sized nails create holes of different shapes and diameter. The holes will leave sharp edges on the back of your work, so be careful. An electric drill (see box below) will make a much neater hole but must be used slowly and carefully.

MAKING HOLES USING EYELET PLIERS (B)

Good eyelet pliers have integral hole punches to make clean holes the exact size for your eyelets. They are also useful for making smaller holes in flat metal. They are very easy and efficient to use, but always follow the manufacturer's instructions.

USING A DRILL

Electric drills are very powerful and potentially dangerous. Never wear loose clothing or jewellery that could get caught in the drill while you work. Wear eye goggles to protect yourself from debris when you use a drill. The drill bit will become hot with use, so keep your hands clear of it for a while. Make sure the cable is safely out of the way of the drill bit and unplug the drill before changing to a different-sized bit. You need to use high-speed steel bits for drilling metal. Stick a little piece of masking tape over the point you are going to drill to stop the drill from wandering.

Do not drill with one hand while holding the material with the other; ideally, secure your work with a vice. This is not always possible with cylindrical objects, so have someone wearing protective gloves to hold your work firmly. When you drill, apply pressure slowly and steadily to prevent the metal catching and tearing. Drilling is much easier to do with a pillar drill, but not many of us have access to one, though you may know someone who does.

USING A NEEDLE FILE (C)

Cutting or adding holes to tin will leave 'burrs' (sharp edges) that need to be smoothed. A needle file, made of high-quality steel, is machined and finished for precision filing and can reach into little corners and holes.

SMOOTHING TIN SURFACES (D)

Wire wool is really useful for finer sanding and smoothing, and particularly for removing varnish, paint and rust. A once-over with wire wool is quite useful to give the smooth, shiny surface of metal a key to hold paint more effectively.

USING SPRAY PAINT (E)

A well-ventilated location – preferably outside – will protect you from paint fumes. Otherwise, open as many windows as possible. Paint small projects in a deep cardboard box, or put down a dustsheet or old newspaper for larger pieces.

Remove any rust with wire wool and give your metal a good wipe-down with white spirit or label remover. Make sure it is completely dry before painting. A primer is unnecessary, but will give you a smoother surface, a stronger colour and a longer-lasting finish. Give the spray paint can a good shake for at least three minutes – this will minimize speckles and splodges.

Apply a thin coat of paint over your whole project, leaving the specified time for drying, and repeat this several times. When you have finished, clean the spray valve by holding the can upside down and spraying until only a clear gas is released. This should prevent clogging. Never stick a pin or wire into the hole.

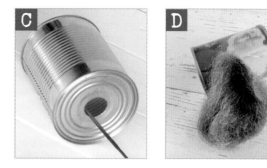

TIP

EMERY PAPER CAN BE USED IN PLACE OF A NEEDLE FILE.

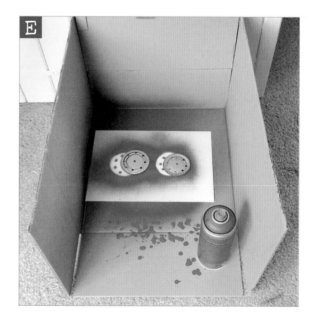

TIP

A COAT OF CLEAR SPRAY VARNISH AFTER PAINTING WILL GIVE YOU A MORE HARD-WEARING FINISH.

BASIC CROCHET TECHNIQUES

HOLDING THE YARN AND HOOK

Keep hold of the work and control the yarn supply with your left hand. Wrap the working yarn under the little finger, over the third finger, under the middle finger and over the index finger. Now use the middle finger to feed the yarn onto the hook (**A**). When you get into the rhythm of crocheting, you will develop your own way of holding the hook. I hold it in an overhand grip (**B**).

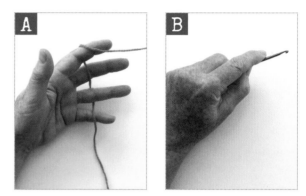

MAKING A SLIP KNOT

Step 1
Make a loop towards the end of your yarn. Make a second loop and pass it through the first.

Step 2
Pull the top loop to tighten the knot. You can make it smaller by pulling one of the tails.

WHERE TO INSERT THE HOOK

If you look closely at your crochet chains you will see that each one is made up of two 'strands' forming a V-shape. You can insert the hook under either one (front or back) (**A**) or both (**B**) of the strands that make up each individual chain. Unless your pattern states otherwise, pick which suits you best, but be consistent.

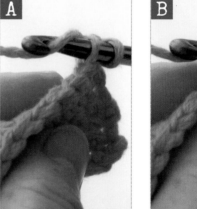

WORKING A FOUNDATION CHAIN (CH ST)

Almost all crochet starts with a foundation (or base) chain, a series of stitches like casting on in knitting. From this, you can work in rows or join the chain into a ring to work in the round.

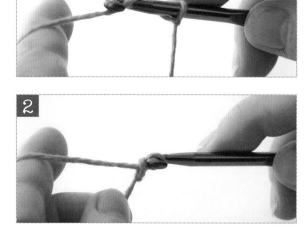

Step 1
Make a slip knot (see facing page), insert the crochet hook and tighten. Hold on to the tail of the yarn with your thumb and middle finger. Wrap the ball end of the yarn clockwise over the hook.

Step 2
Catching the yarn with the hook, draw it towards and through the slip knot to make the first chain.

Step 3
Make further chains in the same way until you have the number required for your pattern. Count the stitches from the front, making sure they are not twisted. Do not count the loop currently on the hook or the initial slip knot.

. . . .

SLIP STITCH (SL ST)

Step 1
Insert the hook into the second chain from the hook. Wrap the yarn anticlockwise over the hook.

Step 2
Pull the yarn through the chain and the loop on the hook in one movement, leaving one loop still on the hook. Work into the next chain in the same way.

DOUBLE CROCHET (DC)

Double crochet makes a taller stitch than slip stitch and creates a dense, firm fabric ideal for making items that need to hold a strong shape. Begin with a foundation chain.

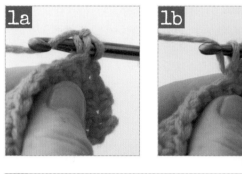

Step 1

Insert the hook into both strands of the second chain from your hook. Wrap the yarn clockwise over the hook, as for slip stitch (see page 125) (1a). Pull the yarn through the chain (there are now two loops on the hook (1b). Wrap the yarn round the hook again.

Step 2

Draw the yarn through both loops, leaving one loop on the hook. This completes the first dc stitch.

Step 3

Insert the hook into the next stitch and repeat steps 1 and 2 to the end of the row. The hook is now at the left end of your crochet. Before starting the next row, turn the work over so that the hook is on the right again and work a turning chain (see facing page).

TENSION SQUARES

Working a tension square helps to guarantee the size of your finished piece. Make at least 10 ch and work a minimum of 10 rows using the stitch, yarn and hook specified in the pattern. Fasten off and pin out flat, pressing if necessary using a hot iron and a damp cloth. Using a tape measure or ruler, check the number of stitches and rows to 1in (2.5cm). If there are more stitches than specified in the pattern, try again with a larger hook. If there are fewer, try a smaller hook.

WORKING TURNING CHAINS

At the beginning of a follow-on row you need to work extra chains to bring the yarn up to the right height for the stitches you are about to work. These extra chains are called 'turning chains'. Without them the row would be too low at one end and your work would become uneven.

The number of chains required depends on the height of the stitch: for double crochet work one or two turning chains and for treble crochet, which is a taller stitch, work three turning chains.

Step 1

Turn the work at the end of a row so that the hook is now on the right with one loop on it. Make a loose turning chain or chains by drawing a loop of yarn through the loop on the hook.

Step 2

For double crochet, work the first stitch of the row into the stitch at the base of the turning chain (2a). For treble crochet, work the first stitch into the fourth stitch of the previous row (2b).

TIP

FOR DOUBLE CROCHET, THE TURNING CHAIN DOES NOT COUNT AS A STITCH BUT FOR TREBLE CROCHET AND OTHER TALLER STITCHES, IT DOES.

JOINING IN NEW YARN

Drop the old yarn just before working the final yarn over of a stitch, make the yarn over using the new yarn and pull it through to complete the stitch. Hold down both tail ends until you have worked the next stitch. There is no need to knot them together.

CHANGING COLOUR

Step 1

Drop the previous colour just before working the final yarn over of a stitch, and use the new colour for the final wrap round the hook.

Step 2

Pull the yarn through so the loop on the hook is in the new colour, ready for the next stitch. Continue working in the new colour.

TIP

TO WORK A WHOLE ROW IN A NEW COLOUR, CHANGE YARN AT THE END OF THE LAST STITCH OF THE PREVIOUS ROW.

FINISHING OFF

Make 1 ch and cut the working yarn leaving a 2–4in (5–10cm) tail. Pull the tail through the loop and tighten to prevent unravelling. Use a yarn needle or small crochet hook to weave the tail through the stitches at the back of your work. Cut the tail flush using sharp scissors.

ELECTRICAL WIRING

You should not take on electric wiring projects unless you are confident you know what you are doing. For the projects in this book you need to know how to wire a plug and a lamp holder correctly and safely – look online for wiring instructions specific to your region.

Preparation is key to safety. Before starting a project, gather all the elements you need together, laying them out in the correct order for assembling. Make sure you've got all the appropriate tools to hand as well and are confident using them.

CABLE AND CORD

For electrical lighting projects you should use three-core cable – this is the safest to use for the projects in this book, as the tin cans and other metal elements are conductive and the earth wire ensures safety from shorting.

You can purchase cord in a wonderful array of coverings and colours these days. Pick one to complement, or to contrast with, your project.

ELECTRICAL WIRING SAFETY
Always be patient – never rush a wiring project. Double-check any wiring before plugging in your lights. If in any doubt, consult a professional before you switch on.

TIP

A QUALIFIED ELECTRICIAN WOULD BE ABLE TO WIRE YOUR PROJECT SAFELY IN LESS TIME THAN IT TAKES YOU TO LEARN HOW. IF IN ANY DOUBT, TAKE YOUR COMPONENTS TO A PROFESSIONAL TO ASSEMBLE.

TEMPLATES

With a little confidence, these templates can be
adapted for your chosen tins. But be inspired: use
your own photographs for the Cress-growing Tin,
or adapt the blossoms for the Blossom Wreath if you
want to add different-shaped flowers or some leaves.

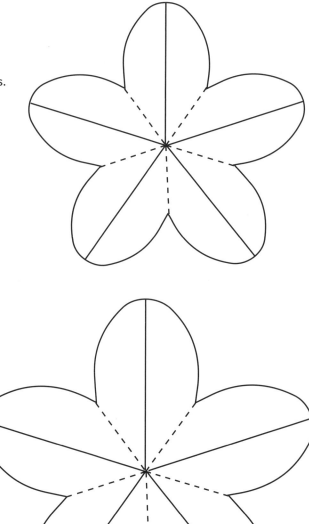

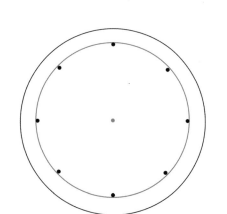

Disc Decorations p.88
Scale to size for your tin lid

Desk Lamp p.52
Scale to fit snuggly inside your tin

Blossom Wreath p.72
Copy at 100%

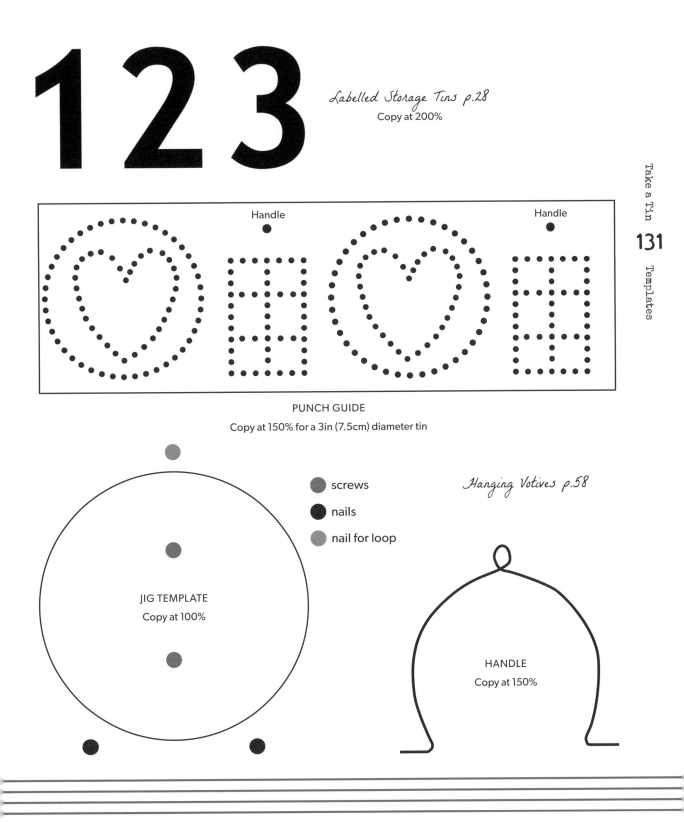

123

Labelled Storage Tins p.28
Copy at 200%

Handle

Handle

PUNCH GUIDE
Copy at 150% for a 3in (7.5cm) diameter tin

● screws
● nails
● nail for loop

Hanging Votives p.58

JIG TEMPLATE
Copy at 100%

HANDLE
Copy at 150%

Picture Frame p.82

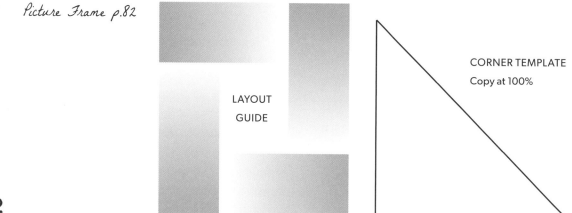

CORNER TEMPLATE
Copy at 100%

LAYOUT

GUIDE

Travel Games p.112

Scale to size for your tin

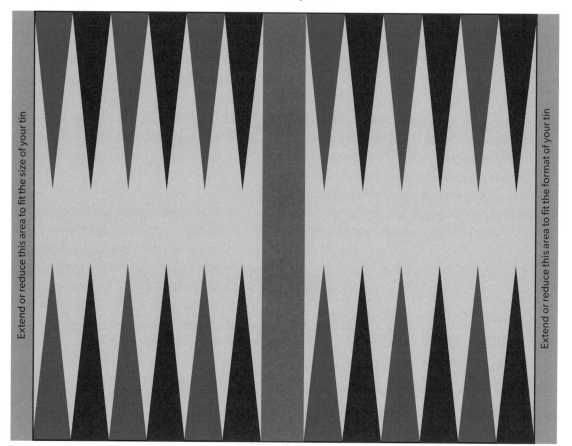

Extend or reduce this area to fit the size of your tin

Extend or reduce this area to fit the format of your tin

CRESS-GROWING
INSTRUCTIONS
AND ENVELOPE
Scale to size for your tin

Cress-growing Kit p.94

Preparation
You don't need to soak the seeds before
sowing – just remove the lid of your tin and
carefully tear open the packet.

Growing your cress
Sprinkle the cress seeds evenly over the
layer of cotton wool. Add enough water to
make it damp but not wet, and place it on a
windowsill. Make sure the cotton wool doesn't
dry out by adding enough water regularly
to keep it moist.

Harvesting
Snip the greens off just above the cotton wool
when they reach 1¾in (4cm) tall.

Storage
Cress can't really be stored, so eat straight
after cutting – in salads, or in a delicious
quail's egg and cress sandwich.

QUAIL'S EGG
Scale to size for your tin

QUAIL'S EGG AND CRESS SANDWICHES

You will need:
4 slices of bread
Freshly cut cress
1 dozen fresh quail's eggs
Soft, unsalted butter
Sea salt and freshly ground black pepper

Lower the eggs gently into a pan of boiling water
and bring back to the boil. Simmer for two minutes,
then drain and leave under cold, running water
until cool enough to peel comfortably – your
yokes should still be slightly moist and the eggs
still warm. Using a knife, roughly mash the eggs
and add a couple of knobs of soft butter. Butter
the slices of bread. Pile the egg mixture onto two
of the slices of bread and sprinkle with freshly cut
cress, sea salt and freshly ground black pepper to
season. Top with the remaining two slices of bread,
trim off the crusts with a sharp bread knife, cut into
triangles or fingers and serve.

RECIPE
Scale to fit inside
your envelope

Suppliers

VINTAGE TINS
sandrascornerstore at etsy

MAGNETS
www.magnetexpert.co.uk

STUFFING
www.dunelm.com

TRIMS, THREADS AND FABRICS
www.brightonsewingcentre.com

YARNS
www.knitrowan.com

ACRYLIC SPRAY PAINTS
www.clarkesofficesupplies.co.uk

ELECTRICAL AND WIRING
www.edwardsandhope.co.uk

EYELETS AND EYELET PUNCHES
www.bicwarehouse.com

TOOLS
www.dockerills.co.uk

WAX, WICKS AND FRAGRANCES
www.randallscandles.co.uk

Acknowledgements

AUTHOR'S ACKNOWLEDGEMENTS
Thank you to Jonathan, Gilda, Virginia, Luana, Robin and everyone at GMC who helped in the production of this book. Thank you to Emma for the beautiful photographs, to Val and Paul for the use of their very special house and to Stacie at Edwards and Hope. Thanks also to Fran and Ben at Egg & Spoon and Chelsea for lovely tins, to Michelle and Matt for their help, to Mop for her critical and encouraging eye. A special thank you to Harrison and to lovely Martha for her martinis. As always, the most thanks to my family and friends. x

GMC PUBLICATIONS would like to thank: Rebecca, Paul, Emma and Guy for lending props. Photo on page 133: © Shutterstock/domnitsky.

Index

B
Blossom Wreath 72–77, 130
Box Pincushion 38–43
Brioche-tin Candles 66–69

C
cables 129
changing colour 128
cleaning 121
colour 128
Cookie-cutter Chimes 78–81
cords 129
Cress-growing Kit 94–97, 133
crochet techniques 124–128
cutting 121

D
Desk Lamp 52–57, 130
Disc Decorations 88–91, 130
double crochet 126, 127
drills 122

E
electrical wiring 129
equipment 118–119, 121, 122, 123

F
finishing off 128
foundation chains 125

H
Heart Votives 58–61, 131
holding the yarn and hook 124
holes 122–123
hooks 124

I
inserting the hook 124

J
joining in new yarn 128

L
Labelled Storage Tins 28–31, 131

M
Magnetic Pinboard 32–37
materials 118, 119
Memory Tin 98–105

N
needle files 123

O
opening tin cans 120

P
paint 123
Pendant Light 62–65
Picture Frame 82–87, 132

Q
Quail's Egg and Cress
Sandwiches (recipe) 133

R
Ring-pull Bracelet 106–111

S
safety 120, 121, 122, 129
scissors 121
slip knots 124
slip stitch 125
smoothing surfaces 123
spray paint 123
suppliers 134

T
techniques 120–129
templates 130–133
tension squares 126
texture 122–123
Tiered Storage Stand 44–49
tin cutting 121
tin opening 120
tin snips 121
tools 118, 119, 121, 122, 123
Travel Games 112–115, 132
turning chains 127

W
working turning chains 127

Y
yarns 124, 128

To place an order, or to request
a catalogue, contact:

GMC Publications Ltd, Castle Place,
166 High Street, Lewes, East Sussex,
BN7 1XU, United Kingdom

Tel: +44 (0)1273 488005
www.gmcbooks.com